CHILDREN
OF THE
WAR YEARS

CHILDHOOD IN BRITAIN
DURING 1939 TO 1945

CHILDREN
— OF THE —
WAR YEARS

CHILDHOOD IN BRITAIN
DURING1939 TO 1945

JANICE ANDERSON

Futura

A Futura Book

First published by Futura in 2008

ISBN: 978-0-7088-0368-4

Produced by Omnipress Limited, UK

Printed in China

Futura
An imprint of
Little, Brown Book Group
100 Victoria Embankment
London EC4Y 0DY

Photo credits: Getty Images

An Hachette Livre UK Company

CONTENTS

WAR COMES TO THE HOME FRONT

The second great war of the 20th century, which broke out in September 1939, engulfed the home populations of most of the countries that got caught up in it. In Europe, millions of men, women and children were killed or wounded and whole cities were devastated.

Because Britain escaped invasion – by a hairsbreadth, as later historians have come to believe – the country as a whole also escaped death and destruction on the same horrifying scale as was experienced in Europe. But the country did not escape unscathed. There were many thousands of deaths, much injury, both physical and psychological, to men, women and children, and much hardship and devastation.

For the children of Britain, the war years were an extraordinary experience. To take the bad statistics first: more than 7,700 children under the age of 16 were killed as a result of enemy action and almost another 7,700 were seriously wounded. Many thousands more were left fatherless, orphaned or without family altogether, as enemy bombing destroyed whole houses and everyone in them. For thousands of children and their families who escaped all this, there were many years of social upheaval, of being moved from one temporary kind of housing to another, of being evacuated, sometimes 'for the duration', to a part of the country many miles from home and family, where social customs were very different from anything they had experienced before.

The surprising thing is the very positive view of the war taken, years later, by the majority of the children who lived through it. Among the positive changes that came out of the war, several radically affected the lives of future generations of children. The war jerked Britain's political leaders out of their complacent acceptance of the living conditions endured by thousands, even

SOME GRIM STATISTICS

While the numbers of children killed and wounded in Britain during World War II make very sad reading, they are, thankfully, small in comparison with the dreadful figures from other countries. The number of Jewish children who perished in the Holocaust exceeded 1 million, while 400,000 Russian children died in the siege of Leningrad (St Petersburg). Several million children died in Germany, where 6 million under-16-year-olds were caught up in the fighting as combatants and civilians; 5,500 children were killed in Hamburg in 1943 in devastating Allied raids. The world still does not know how many Japanese children were killed outright, died later or were born malformed in mind and body when the Allies dropped atom bombs on Hiroshima and Nagasaki in 1945.

millions of poor, working-class people. The great evacuation schemes of the war brought Britain's middle classes face to face with the reality of life in the inner cities, where so many children knew nothing of indoor plumbing, or of having regular baths, regular changes of clothes, or hair free of nits and parasites... The result was the Welfare State, developed from the Beveridge Report that was accepted by Parliament at a time when the country was fighting grimly for its very survival.

BREAKDOWN OF CLASS

The war also brought about a great breaking down of class barriers. While parents became aware of the great divide existing between the classes in Britain, their children found that their horizons were considerably widened. For children from the inner cities, there was the amazing discovery that beyond the city streets was a different world, one with many open, green spaces and farms where men and women worked to produce food. If a boy or girl evacuated from an inner city was reasonably lucky, they might find foster parents who would take them roller skating, let them join the Boy Scouts or Girl Guides, and spend their summer holidays on one of the country's beaches still free of barbed wire. No wonder many children returned only reluctantly to their families at the war's end.

And there was plenty of horizon-widening for middle-class children, too. When schoolgirl Joan Elliott's father was

▲ *Going to a New Home*
Some of the thousands of children who were evacuated to the Sussex coast after the start of World War II now await transport to their new reception areas in the Home Counties.

moved to Scottish Command, the whole family went, including their maid, their grandmother and her maid, to stay in a small village outside Edinburgh. Joan and her siblings discovered a new freedom playing on various pieces of green land where their special playmates were a family of boys from 'the wrong side of the tracks'. The boys taught her many scurrilous rhymes that played a considerable part in her education.

Education was, in fact, another part of children's lives that underwent many changes during the war. It was not just that school life was turned upside down by the upheavals of evacuation and the calling up of so many young teachers. The war also accelerated changes in the education system that had been begun in the 1930s. The great Education Act of 1944 was the result of many years' planning, which did not let up

because 'there was a war on' – the great wartime excuse for not allowing things to happen.

MAKE DO AND MEND

But it must not be forgotten that there was, indeed, a war on, and one in which children were involved from the very beginning. Children were brought into all the great wartime campaigns, such as 'Dig For Victory' and 'Make Do and Mend'. As the war progressed and the children became old enough – as young as 12, in many cases – they were also brought into civil defence work and even into the junior corps of the armed services.

Children were also the government's major target of one of its greatest wartime concerns: keeping the nation well fed and healthy. Throughout the war, babies and children were ensured a good supply of fresh milk and eggs, cod liver oil and orange juice, and the Ministry of Food kept up a steady barrage of information, including its own BBC radio programme, aimed at ensuring that Britain's children enjoyed – perhaps not the right word, given some of the not very palatable recipes dreamed up by the Ministry – a sound, nutritious diet.

On the whole, the nation did pretty well by its children during World War II. It is noticeable in wartime photographs that most children look healthy, well fed and warmly clothed. As for the children of the war years themselves, the memories may be mixed, but the overwhelming memory is of a time when everyone did their bit, and did it with their neighbours and their friends in a remarkably cheerful spirit.

◀

Bombed Inn
14 August 1945: Boys clearing rubble on the bombed site of the Hopskotch Inn, near Euston station, London. The site is to be turned into a junior club for children by the Save The Children Fund.

POPULAR CULTURE IN 1939

Popular Songs

Over the Rainbow, performed by Judy Garland
Moonlight Serenade, performed by Glenn Miller
Strange Fruit, performed by Billie Holiday
When the Saints go Marching in, performed by Louis Armstrong
Jeepers Creepers, performed by Al Donohue
Begin the Beguine by Chick Henderson with Joe Loss and his band
At the Woodchoppers' Ball, by Woody Herman
Beer Barrel Polka, by Will Glahe
There'll Always be an England, by Ross Parker and Harry Par-Davies

High-grossing films

Gone with the Wind, starring Vivien Leigh and Clark Gable
The Wizard of Oz, starring Judy Garland
Jesse James, starring Tyrone Power, Henry Fonda, Nancy Kelly and Randolph Scott
Mr Smith Goes to Washington, starring James Stewart, Jean Arthur and Claude Rains
The Hunchback of Notre Dame, starring Charles Laughton, Sir Cedric Hardwicke and Maureen O'Hara

EVACUATION

*Although relatively few people were killed or seriously wounded during
German air bombing attacks on Britain during World War I,
the number of dead – about 1,400 – was enough to make everyone realise that warfare
in the 20th century would inevitably involve those at home
as much as those in the armed forces.*

▲ *ID Check*
*A little girl examines her companion's identity tag as they and other children get ready to be
evacuated from London to the safety of the countryside.*

WHY IMMEDIATE EVACUATION?

The government began its evacuation scheme as a military measure, designed to prevent panic and devastating loss of morale and to get people away quickly from the ferocious attack expected from the enemy immediately after any declaration of war. As early as 1931, ARP committee members were told by experts to expect 3,500 tons of bombs to be dropped on Britain in the first 24 hours of war, with about 600 tons being dropped every day thereafter. This scale of bombing, said the experts, was likely to result in casualties on an unprecedented scale: up to 60,000 dead and 120,000 wounded on the first day, with up to 66,000 dead and 130,000 wounded every week thereafter. Such atrocities as the 1937 bombing of the Spanish city of Guernica by German planes during the Spanish Civil War reinforced these appalling predictions.

1939
JANUARY

4 President Roosevelt calls for an increase in the US defence budget.

9 Hitler reopens the Reichstag building, which was destroyed by fire in 1933.

10 Chamberlain meets with Mussolini in Rome.

17 Germans pass a law forbidding Jews to drive cars.

19 The former president of the Reichstag is dismissed by Hitler for suggesting that Germany's rearmament programme threatens the economy.

24 Gestapo officer Reinhard is asked to speed up the evacuation of Jews from Germany.

30 Hitler threatens the Jewish race during his Reichstag speech.

FEBRUARY

10 Poland closes the Danzig Corridor to German road and rail traffic.

14 The German battleship *Bismarck* is launched.

23 Jews are ordered to hand in any precious metals or stones.

27 The UK and France recognise Franco's Spanish government.

Even as the peace treaty that settled affairs after World War I was being signed, Europe's governments and politicians were considering how best to save their civilian populations in the all too likely event of another war. Plans to evacuate civilians from major cities and industrial areas were first officially discussed in Britain in the early 1920s, when a special Air Raid Precautions (ARP) committee began investigating the pros and cons of air raid defence.

Two essential points were obvious from the outset. First, it would be very bad for national morale if thousands of people were killed or seriously injured in the first days of the war, as most experts expected. Evacuation would have to be done swiftly and, if possible, before war broke out. Second, in a parliamentary democracy people could not be ordered to move away from their homes and neighbourhoods to places that might be safer in the event of war. They would have to be persuaded. Since any worthwhile war effort would grind to a halt if major cities and important industrial areas were to be deprived of their working populations, total evacuation was not possible. This meant that evacuation would have to be selective as well as voluntary.

1939

MARCH

13 Berlin demands the dismissal of anti-Nazi ministers from the government.

15 Hitler marches into Prague, effectively bringing about the end of Czechoslovakia.

20 In protest to Germany's invasion of Prague, the US recall their ambassador from Berlin.

25 The second cartoon to feature Happy Rabbit (the prototype Bugs Bunny), *Prest-O Change-O*, is released.

28 Franco takes Madrid and the Spanish Civil War ends.

31 Britain and France join forces and agree to defend Poland against any aggressors.

APRIL

3 Germany makes plans to invade Poland.

7 Italy invades Albania.

11 Hungary leaves the League of Nations.

20 Hitler celebrates his 50th birthday with a military parade in Berlin, and the day is declared a national holiday.

26 The British government proposes compulsory military service.

28 Hitler revokes a 10-year non-aggression pact with Poland.

Britain was slower than other countries in Europe to make serious plans for evacuating their population in the event of war. The early work of the ARP committee was desultory and lacking in in-depth planning; very little thought was given at this stage to what should happen to people once they had been evacuated. But as the 1930s progressed, people began to concentrate much more seriously on the matter. National Socialist Germany, led by Adolf Hitler, was becoming increasingly belligerent and militaristic. Then came the Spanish Civil War with its terrible devastation and loss of life.

In July 1938, two years after France had issued evacuation guidance to its citizens, the British government delivered to all households *The Householders' Handbook*, in which it was suggested that, in the event of war, such members of the household as children, elderly people, invalids and pets should be sent, if possible, to stay with friends and relatives in the country. Much more serious planning was taking place behind the scenes. A Committee on Evacuation, chaired by Sir John Anderson, the Lord Privy Seal, was set up in May 1938, by which time it was clear that, even though any evacuation scheme would be voluntary, the government must be in control of evacuation plans in order to avoid the panic and chaos seen in Spain. It was also clear by now that the emphasis should be on evacuating children (with their mothers in the case of very young children) from the danger areas.

▶

A group of evacuee children carrying their belongings in suitcases and bags as they stand at the station, ready to start their new lives away from the dangers of London during the bomb blitzes. One girl looks back for the last time before boarding her train.

By this time, non-government organisations were also swinging into action. Prominent among these was the Women's Voluntary Service (WVS), formed by the redoubtable Stella, Marchioness of Reading, in June 1938. Although its founding purpose was the recruitment of women into the civil defence services, the WVS turned out to be one of the nation's greatest civilian wartime assets. Within a few weeks of its founding, the WVS had set up an Evacuation Committee with members including representatives of the Girl Guides and the Women's Institutes (WI). This committee appointed WVS Evacuation Officers to work with local authorities to coordinate the billeting of evacuees in every county in the land that was likely to receive evacuees. The inclusion of the Girl Guides in the WVS evacuation scheme meant that children were able to help other children, for many of the Girl Guides meeting the great columns of schoolchildren evacuated from the danger areas in September 1939 were themselves 'teenagers' (a term not yet invented) and therefore still legally children.

◀
September 1939: A group of children evacuated from Salford to Blackpool.

War suddenly seemed very close indeed in September 1938, when Germany laid claim to the Sudetenland, which lay on their border with Czechoslovakia, a country with which Britain had treaty obligations. At the height of the Munich Crisis, as this incident came to be called, the government was ready to assist with the evacuation, on a voluntary basis, of 2 million people, a quarter of them schoolchildren, from London alone. By the end of September, many parents of school-age children in London were receiving letters from head teachers that, far from dealing with matters of education, were asking them to send their children to school with neatly packed and clearly labelled luggage, and with sufficient food (listed in the letter) to last them for a couple of days. They were to be evacuated, mostly by train, bus or coach, but also by steamer and ferry boat, with fellow pupils and their teachers, for an unspecified time – and, in many cases, to an unspecified place.

Fortunately, this crisis was resolved without war, the Prime Minister, Neville Chamberlain, coming back from Germany at the end of September with a 'piece of paper' that promised 'peace for our time'. Although few believed that the 'time' available for peace was very long, at least the Munich Crisis gave the country a chance to rehearse an admittedly rudimentary evacuation scheme and to iron out the worst of the flaws – one of the greatest of which was the identification of suitable billets – the rehearsal had thrown up.

The British Government's evacuation scheme, passed on to local authorities at the beginning of 1939, was based on dividing the country into three areas. The danger zones, called 'Evacuation Areas', included the capital, large urban areas, industrial regions including Birmingham, Salford, Newcastle and Gateshead and the important dockyards of the Clyde around Glasgow. And important major military installations such as the

Medway towns in Kent and Rosyth in Scotland, thought most at risk from a major aerial attack in the first days of the war. The decision to omit the major Devon naval base of Plymouth from this list was taken because Plymouth was thought to be too far away to come within range of German 'first strike' attacks. This serious miscalculation was not put right until after the heavy raids on Plymouth in March and April 1941.

'Reception Areas' were the parts of the country, mostly rural and coastal areas, thought to be out of range of attack, to which evacuees would be sent. Once these areas were decided upon, the first task of local authorities, aided by such voluntary organisations as the WVS and the WI, was to assess the amount of 'surplus accommodation' available for evacuees. 'Neutral Areas' were those that neither sent nor received evacuees.

The government's evacuation scheme

The government's evacuation scheme identified four groups likely to be caught up in evacuation. One of the four groups included those individuals and families able to afford to make their own, private arrangements for leaving the Evacuation Areas. It is thought that about 2 million people quietly left the danger areas for the peace of western coastal resorts and rural Britain, staying with relatives or in hotels and guest houses, in the months before war was declared. Thousands more left the country altogether, many of them taking ships to the United States. In both these groups were many children. The evacuation of children by ship to the United States came to an abrupt end in 1940, with the sinking of a ship carrying a large group of children to America.

This left three groups where some form of government assistance would be necessary: businesses and private companies, the government and civil service, and – probably needing the most financial assistance – children, their mothers and invalids. This last group, estimated to total about 4 million, would come largely from working class areas, such as the East End of London, and the inner, more crowded parts of the great industrial cities of the north of England and of Scotland.

◀

London, 1 September, 1939: children from the English Martyrs Roman Catholic School boarding a train at Waterloo Station before being evacuated to the safety of the countryside.

1939

MAY

Comic book superhero Batman, created by Bob Kane, makes his first appearance.

12 Germany attacks Polish property in Danzig.

22 Germany and Italy sign 'the pact of steel'.

31 Germany and Denmark sign a 10-year non-aggression pact.

JUNE

4 The SS *St Louis*, a ship carrying a cargo of 907 Jewish refugees, including over 400 women and children, is denied permission to dock in Florida.

7 Germany signs non-aggression pacts with Latvia and Estonia. The start of deportation of Jews to Poland.

23 France and Turkey sign a mutual defence treaty.

JULY

9 Winston Churchill proposes a military alliance with Russia.

17 Poland decides to declare its opposition in case Germany attacks Danzig.

31 Polish customs officials are ordered to leave Danzig. Poland responds with economic sanctions.

1939

AUGUST

15 MGM's *The Wizard of Oz*, starring Judy Garland, premieres in Hollywood.

20 Hitler announces that 'the destruction of Poland will start on Saturday morning' in a speech to his generals.

23 Hitler and Stalin sign a non-aggression pact.

24 Poland mobilises her forces ready for war.

25 Poland and Britain sign a mutual assistance treaty.

30 Every household in London receives a pack providing details of an evacuation scheme; those affected are mostly children.

SEPTEMBER

1 Germany invades Poland. Italy, Norway, Finland, Switzerland, Spain and Ireland proclaim their neutrality.

3 Britain, France, Australia and New Zealand declare war on Germany.
The British passenger ship the *SS Athenia* is sunk by German submarine U-30. German forces penetrate the Polish corridor. Belgium declares its neutrality.

4 Napal declares war on Germany.
The British Royal Air Force attacks the German Navy.

Evacuating the children of Britain from the Evacuation Areas depended on the meshing together of a great network of individuals and organisations. The schools and their teaching staff would be evacuated with their pupils, and the railway companies provided the trains – and the timetables – to shift hundreds of thousands of bewildered children to safety. Organisations like the WVS and local authorities sought out the 'surplus accommodation' in the Reception Areas, that would, if suitable, become the billets for those children, their mothers and their teachers. People offering accommodation to evacuees were paid a sufficient amount to cover their costs. Well before war was declared in September 1939, local authorities in the Reception Areas were able to tell the government that they could make accommodation available for not far short of 5 million people. Evacuation was fast becoming an experiment in social reorganisation on an unprecedented scale.

One of the government's major tasks was to persuade parents to send their children out of the Evacuation Areas. Women, because there were so many more of them at home, were the main target of government propaganda. In the Reception Areas posters began appearing in the spring of 1939 asking for women to help with the evacuation service: '*Offer your services to your local council*', exhorted the posters. In the Evacuation Areas the posters were aimed at mothers. By early 1939, the 1938 *Householders' Handbook*'s mild suggestion that evacuation would be a good idea had turned into something much more direct: '*MOTHERS Send Them Out of London, Give them a chance of greater safety and health*', the wording of a poster used in London, was typical of those with a similar message being displayed in Britain's major cities.

Most mothers did not need posters to force them into thinking about whether evacuation was a good idea or not. For months, everyday family life was being moved on to a war footing. As far back as September 1938, all adults and children (but not babies, for whom gas masks were not provided until the outbreak of war), had been practising using the smelly and unattractive gas masks that had been delivered to every adult and child in the country during the Munich Crisis. By May 1939, every mother who wished to be evacuated with her small children should have registered at her local maternity or child welfare centre, making it clear at the time if she wished her older children to be taken out of school to go with her.

The 'evacuate or not' decision was very difficult for those mothers whose children were all of school age. Such children were expected to be evacuated with their schools and teachers, so their mothers would have to wave them goodbye from the school gate. There was a major evacuation rehearsal in most evacuation areas in the country on 28 August 1939. From 6 a.m. children began arriving at their schools dressed ready to go, labels on their coats and on the single suitcases or bags, packed with a suggested list of clothes, just one toy per child, and a parcel of food, and with the boxes containing their gas masks hanging round their necks.

On 31 August, while desperate negotiations with Hitler were still going on in a last-ditch effort to prevent war, the Ministry of Health announced that, 'as a precautionary measure,' the evacuation of school children and other priority classes would start the next day, 1 September 1939. On paper, the evacuation, code-named Operation Pied Piper, looked well organised. In reality, there were such crowds of children milling about at railway stations – both mainline and suburban stations had to be brought into use to cope with the numbers – over the three days the evacuation lasted that the carefully worked out timetables went by the board. Operation Pied Piper intended that whole schools would be evacuated en masse, but in the chaotic

conditions, classes got separated and groups of children were loaded onto the first available train and sent off to what, in many cases, was an unknown destination. They arrived many hours later, tired, hungry, dirty and frightened.

PACKING EVACUATION BAGS

The mothers of children who were to be evacuated with their schools were sent a list suggesting what their children should take with them. Since the list was very basic – a change of underwear, night clothes, one pair of shoes or plimsolls, stockings and socks, toilet gear including toothbrush, towel and soap, plus handkerchiefs and one warm coat – the average middle- or working-class family had little trouble with it. For poor mothers – and, since some of the poorest parts of Britain's inner cities were to the fore in the Evacuation Areas – fulfilling the list's requirements put them into debt. Children turning up at assembly points with their possessions in a pillow case, shoe bag, cardboard box or brown paper parcel was an early indication of the depth of child poverty in Britain that the wartime evacuations revealed.

▲
Wartime Reunion
Parents from London are reunited with their
evacuated children in Saffron Walden, Essex,
22 October 1939: nearly 1,000 parents attended
the reunion party, hosted by the Mayor of the
town.

▶
Small Evacuee
Young Freddie Somer of Winton Street School
arrives at King's Cross Station, London, but is
distressed by the thought of being relocated.

April 1944: A group of London children looking out of a railway carriage window en route to a place of safety.

In the event, total evacuation of children to safe Reception Areas was never achieved in 1939, and most Reception Areas received far fewer children than they had been led to expect. Where some 80 per cent of mothers interviewed during the Munich Crisis had said that they planned to evacuate their children in the event of war, one year later a much calmer – or perhaps more fatalistic – view seemed the norm. Just over a third of the children expected to be evacuated from London were sent away from the metropolis during 1939, 377,000 of them with their teachers.

In the Birmingham industrial area, Rotherham, Sheffield and other large cities, even fewer children were sent away to escape enemy action than in London. These low figures may have been a result of indifferent publicity for the evacuation scheme by some local authorities. It could also have been because local people did not like the government's arrangements for them. The city of Sheffield, for instance, wanted to send their children into Derbyshire, but the government insisted on Lincolnshire – further away from Sheffield and a lot nearer to Hitler's Luftwaffe. A lack of simple, joined-up

1939
SEPTEMBER

5 The US declares its neutrality.
6 South Africa declares war on Germany.
10 Canada declares war on Germany.
17 The Soviet Union invades Poland and occupies eastern Polish territories.
20 First air battle between the German Luftwaffe and the RAF over Germany.
27 Warsaw surrenders following heavy bombardment.
29 Germany and Russia divide up Poland.
30 Polish government set up in exile in Paris.

OCTOBER

1 Polish Navy surrenders.
8 All Polish secondary schools and colleges are closed, and young men forcibly drafted into the Polish Army.
9 Hitler orders preparations for a massive offensive against France, Holland and Belgium.
12 Deportation of Austrian and Czech Jews to Poland begins.
17 Hitler begins his euthanasia of sick and disabled people and declares that the area of the Reich is to be 'rid of Jews, Poles and other unwanted elements'.

A ROYAL EXAMPLE

The daughters of King George VI and Queen Elizabeth were aged 13 and 9 in September 1939. Setting an example to the nation, the Queen refused to send her daughters to Canada, as the Dutch royal family had done, at the outbreak of war. She did, however, keep them out of London. The princesses spent much of the war at Windsor Castle, where the dungeons provided a safe refuge from the Blitz. During her radio broadcast to 'the children of the Empire' during the BBC's *Children's Hour* in October 1940, Princess Elizabeth spoke of the sadness of being separated from her parents. Although the King and Queen spent much of their daytime in London at Buckingham Palace, which was bombed several times during the war, they spent most of their nights at Windsor Castle. The royal princesses saw much more of their parents than many children during the war.

1939

OCTOBER

30 In Britain a white paper is published regarding the horrors of Nazi concentration camps.

NOVEMBER

1 The Polish corridor and Danzig now officially passed over to the German Reich, along with all the territories ceded to Poland under the terms of the Treaty of Versailles in 1919.

3 The neutrality bill put in place by the USA is amended to allow Britain and France to obtain arms.

8 Two British agents of the SIS are captured by German forces.
An assassination attempt on Hitler fails.

23 Armed merchant ship HMS *Rawalpindi* sunk by German warships *Gneisenau* and *Scharnhorst* in the Atlantic.

29 Russia ends diplomatic relations with Finland.

30 Russia invades Finland.

DECEMBER

1 *Graf Spee* sinks British Steamer *Doric Star* in the Atlantic.

2 La Guardia airport opens for business in New York.

13 *Graf Spee* is spotted off the River Plate estuary near Montevideo.

thinking resulted in many ill-conceived evacuations, such as the dispatching of a large group of Catholic and Irish children from the poorest parts of Liverpool into Calvinist North Wales.

Things were less than ideal in the Reception Areas, too. For many children, the memory of their arrival in the place where they were perhaps to remain for a long time, was confusing and frightening. So, far from being assigned directly to suitable billets, children found themselves lined up in school halls, village halls and even on railway station platforms with those offering billets free to choose those children they liked the look of, or perhaps, if it was a rural community, because they were boys who could be useful labour on the farms. Recalling such scenes in later life, people used terms like 'cattle market' to describe the business. Many people offering billets could take only one or two children, so that families with several brothers and sisters found themselves separated from each other.

Of course, very many children were happy with their new foster parents, often calling them 'Auntie' and 'Uncle', perhaps staying with them for the duration of the war and keeping up regular contact for years after. For many inner city children, life in the country, where the changing seasons were noticeable in a way hardly seen in inner city areas, was a revelation.

As well as those British children caught up in evacuation, the government and local authorities also had to deal with British nationals coming into the country from outside the mainland. Foremost among these were the people of the Channel Islands. In fact, although the Channel Islands had been included in general evacuation discussions, no serious plans had been laid for evacuation to Britain. In June 1940, when the dreadful day came on which the British government had to inform the Channel Islands that they could not be defended from the Germans, the people of the Channel Islands were given less than two days to organise the evacuation of their children and the mothers of children under school age. In 10 days at the end of June some 29,000 islanders were able to cram onto the small fleet of ships that took them to relative safety in England. Many of the children were sent away with their schools, and did not see their parents again for five long years. In the single pieces of luggage each child was allowed to carry, they could pack just one toy.

The Channel Islands evacuees landed first at Weymouth and were then dispersed to various places in west and north England and to Scotland. Eventually, some 36,000 Channel Islanders reached Britain as evacuees. They were cut off from any meaningful contact with their families still on the islands, apart from a few, heavily censored letters, sent via the Red Cross. In England, a Channel Islands Committee helped maintain the islanders as a community.

▲
January 1941: An inn at Camberley, Surrey, which has been converted into a nursery school and billeting centre for 3,000 of the mothers and children evacuated from London.

▲

19 February 1943: Carol Griffin, wounded in an air raid on a school in Lewisham, reads a book with Diana Knight, as they prepare to be evacuated from London during World War II.

The first great World War II evacuation in Britain, in September 1939, began to fall apart when the expected air assaults from Germany did not come. In the months of the Phoney War, as the strangely quiet opening months of the war came to be called, mothers and children began to drift back home. Many children were very unhappy in the alien environments of their billets, and begged their parents to take them home, and expectant mothers and those with babies were bored and lonely. Despite a change of tone in the government's poster-based propaganda campaign, which now called on mothers to 'Leave Them Where They Are', parents were soon taking their children home in ever-increasing numbers. A second attempt at another wave of evacuation in December 1939 met with a poor response.

After the major evacuation of September 1939, there were other, rather smaller waves of evacuation in Britain during the war, most notably after the start of the Blitz in 1940 and then again during the V1 flying bomb (or 'doodlebugs') and V2 rocket attacks in 1944–45. The V weapon attacks began just a week after the D-Day landings in France in June 1944. They were so serious and caused such damage and loss of life that an evacuation scheme for children from southern England was very quickly put into effect.

Mary Murphy, who was just five in 1944, was evacuated from Chingford in Essex to Weston-super-Mare, right on the other side of England in Somerset. Here, she and her friends joined up with evacuee children from London's East End to have mud fights under the pier with local gangs of children. The mud was thick and smelly, and they all had to be hosed down when they got back to their billets.

'After two weeks, our landlady had had enough of us and we were sent back to London in disgrace. We didn't mind because she was grumpy and the food was awful.'

While evacuation undoubtedly saved lives, its long-term effect was unexpected – no less than the creation in Britain of the Welfare State, with its associated National Health Service and other state benefit schemes.

'Grannie' Norris pours tea for some of the evacuees she looked after during WW II. She received the BEM (British Empire Medal) for her 'unremitting care' of a large number of London evacuee children.

▼

▲

August 1950: The village of Droxford became the Allied Invasion headquarters for two days in June 1944. Inhabitants were likely to meet Churchill during their daily routines, and young Christopher McIntosh here once encountered Jan Smuts.

Many of the children evacuated to mainly middle-class homes in quiet towns and country villages came from the poorest slums of Britain's inner cities. Comfortably housed, well-fed and warmly clothed middle-class people were suddenly confronted by children from a world of poverty and deprivation that they thought had vanished with the Victorian age. There were many children who had never encountered an indoor lavatory, never held a fork and knife and seldom, if ever, had a bath. Some of them were still being sewn into heavy (or even paper) underwear at the beginning of winter, expecting not to be cut out of it until the spring. There were reports of children arriving at their Reception Area greeting place with footwear that consisted only of the uppers, the soles having worn away. More than one school used as a greeting point had to be fumigated after the nit- and parasite-infected evacuee children had been moved on. Middle-class Britain was utterly appalled.

Despite being involved in a terrible war, the British government moved into action on a new front: social welfare. In 1941 the government asked the economist Sir William Beveridge to head a committee looking into the way in which a system of social welfare might be set up in Britain. The Beveridge Report, titled *Social Insurance and Allied Services*, which was published in December 1942 and accepted by the government in most of its main points in February 1943, became the foundation on which was built the post-war welfare state.

Home Front evacuation in Britain officially ended on 2 July 1945. The official homecoming for evacuated children, which the government had actually begun preparing for since 1943, began two months before this and although many children had already returned there were still several thousand, including those evacuated during the V1 and V2 attacks, to be returned to their homes and families. It is estimated that some 8 million people, including children, mothers of small children, disabled people and refugees from abroad, were evacuated from Britain's cities during World War II.

1939
DECEMBER

14 Russia is expelled from the League of Nations.
25 Hitler makes a personal visit to inspect his troops on the Western Front.

POPULAR CULTURE IN 1940

Popular Songs

In the Mood by Glenn Miller
Frenesi by Artie Shaw
Only Forever by Bing Crosby
I'll Never Smile Again by Tommy Dorsey
When You Wish Upon a Star by Cliff Edwards (Ukulele Ike)
A Nightingale Sang in Berkeley Square by Glenn Miller
Blueberry Hill by Gene Autry

High-grossing films

Pinocchio, Disney animation
Fantasia, Disney animation
Boom Town, starring Clark Gable and Spencer Tracy
Rebecca, starring Laurence Olivier and Joan Fontaine
Sante Fe Trail, starring Errol Flynn

JANUARY

8 Rationing begins in Britain. Finland scores victory against Russia on the Karelian Front.

THE EFFECTS OF WAR
ON FAMILY LIFE

World War II affected every aspect of life in Britain, from the cradle to the grave.
By the war's end, the nation's idea of what the average British family should be like,
and what its place in society should be, had changed markedly.

The first step in creating a family – giving birth to a child – while it was, of course, surrounded by practical problems in wartime, also led to much heart-searching about the standards of maternity care in the country in general, so that immediately after the war, the provision of well-ordered, nationwide maternity services was a major element in the development of the National Health Service. Many expectant mothers, evacuated to the country where maternity services were a good deal more patchy, if they existed at all, than in the country's large urban areas, found themselves giving birth in improvised maternity units without anaesthetics (which had to be saved for operations).

As the Blitz began, expectant mothers who had been evacuated to country houses hastily converted into maternity homes, could count themselves fortunate, whatever the quality of care available. At least they were not having to give birth, probably while wearing a tin hat, to the sound of air-raid sirens followed by the 'crump' of bombs landing nearby – or, as in the case of Southampton's general hospital on the first night of the many air raids on the city, by the light of a hurricane lamp, with another mother and her newborn baby pushed for safety under the delivery table. Even more appallingly memorable for some mothers was giving birth in the London Underground during an air raid.

For infants and older children, the arrival of the family's gas masks was probably their first practical indication of the fact that family life would not be the same in wartime as it had been up till now. The government was concerned that everyone should have a gas mask, originally called 'respirators', because it seemed very probable that the enemy's first attack would be accompanied by the use of the mustard and chlorine gases that had caused such appalling damage on the Front in World War I.

Children aged between two and five were provided with strangely shaped multi-coloured masks that someone in authority presumably thought would be more acceptable if they were called 'Mickey Mouse' gas masks. Older children were given the same unwieldy and unattractive gas masks as adults. It was not until October 1939 that babies were issued with their own gas masks, which looked like haversack-shaped bags with a perspex visor and with a set of bellows that mothers had to keep pumping to get air in the bag.

▲ *1940: A trap door in the living room floor provides an additional entrance to the cellar during air raids.*

1940

JANUARY

10 Belgium and Holland uncover plans of a German invasion.

16 Hitler delays attacking West until the spring.

30 Hitler speaks out at the Berlin Sportpalast, and declares that the first phase of the war is complete with the destruction of Poland.

FEBRUARY

2 Big Russian offensive on the Karelian front.

7 Walt Disney releases his second full-length animated film: *Pinocchio*.

9 Fighting breaks out on the Mannerheim Line in Finland.

16 299 British prisoners freed from the German ship *Altmark*.

20 Russia and Finland begin new peace talks.

MARCH

2 Elmer Fudd makes his debut in the short *Elmer's Candid Camera*.

13 Finland signs a peace treaty with Russia.

18 Hitler and Mussolini meet at Brennero. 'Il Duce' declares that Italy is now ready to join the war against Britain and France.

1940

APRIL

9 Hitler invades Denmark and Norway in operation *Weserübung*.

10 First battle of Narvik between Royal Navy and *Kriegsmarine*.

13 Second battle of Narvik, resulting in Royal Navy victory. Eight German destroyers are sunk.

14 The Enigma code is broken by British intelligence operatives at Bletchley Park, England.

22 Inter-Allied Supreme War council meets in Paris.

28 The Allied Supreme War Council of France and Britain decides neither will enter into a separate peace agreement with Germany.

MAY

1 Over 4,000 Norwegian troops surrender at Lillehammer.

10 Germany invades France, Belgium, Luxembourg and Netherlands. Neville Chamberlain resigns as British Prime Minister and is succeeded by Winston Churchill.

13 German aerial raid on Rotterdam.
Britain begins recruitment for Local Defence Volunteers; many of those who are too young or too old to be in the real army flock to enrol.

Everyone was advised to practise wearing their gas masks for at least 15 minutes every day. Mothers had to oversee their children's practice because they might not have time to help their children as well as themselves and their babies in the event of a gas attack. All schoolchildren were required to take their gas masks to school, where regular gas mask practices were held in the first weeks of the war. While some schoolboys might have found wearing gas masks great fun, even 'smashing', for many children, wearing the rubber-smelling, claustrophobia-inducing gas masks remained their most unpleasant memory of the war.

As if struggling with their gas masks was not enough, children now found that their homes had become rather gloomy places. Much of their parents' blackout arrangements involved putting black fabric, pieces of heavy cardboard or even black paint over skylights, fan lights and other openings that had to be covered but which it was too impracticable to uncover every morning. Since ARP wardens were very quick to bang on the family front door and shout at parents if the smallest

GAS MASKS

Forty-four million gas masks were distributed in Britain before the outbreak of war. Wearing the gas masks was never made compulsory, although at the beginning of the war it was an offence to leave home without one, and the government contented itself with issuing posters with warnings like 'Hitler will send no warning, so carry your gas mask with you at all times'. One of the most familiar objects in photographs of children during the September 1939 evacuation is the gas mask in its canvas box strung round every child's neck. The gas masks are conspicuous by their absence in photos of later evacuations. In fact, when it very soon became clear that there were going to be no gas attacks from the enemy, people began leaving their masks at home. Schoolchildren, who did not have this option – they might be sent home to get them if they arrived at school without them – soon began to find other uses for the canvas boxes, such as carrying their sandwiches to school in them.

27 June 1941: Children at Cosway Street School, Marylebone, London, trying on their gas masks during a gas instruction lesson.

▼

chink of light was showing, and since people could be fined for consistently showing a light at night, everyone became very careful to observe the blackout properly. Even where a window could be adequately blacked-out with heavy curtains, it might also be criss-crossed with sticky tape or covered with wire net to stop the glass flying about in the event of a bombing raid.

As well as putting up blackout materials, many householders at the start of the war also tried to make their houses as gas-proof as possible. The government advised covering outside doors with heavy hangings, such as carpets, or at least putting heavy draught-excluders at their bases and

covering over fireplaces inside. Such things were so very inconvenient to live with that most householders preferred to make do with their gas masks.

There were other, more practical things that children noticed took up a lot of their parents' time. While mother might be busy round the house, clearing the understairs cupboard so that it could become an emergency air-raid shelter, getting in emergency stocks of torch batteries (soon very hard to find in the shops), candles and blankets and filling kitchen cupboards with emergency rations, father might be outside in the garden building a very strange object indeed. This was the Anderson Shelter.

Nursery school children at play wearing gas masks during World War II.

The Anderson Shelter, named not after Sir John Anderson, the Home Secretary of the day, as is generally believed, but after Dr David Anderson, the engineer who invented it, was an ingenious solution to a serious problem: how to give ordinary people adequate protection from bombs. Households with an annual income below £250 were given their shelters free of charge. The Anderson Shelter was a corrugated steel construction intended to act as a strong roof erected over a deep hole dug in the garden. The earth from the hole was often put over the shelter, to act as extra protection. Many householders soon began planting vegetables on their Anderson Shelter's roof. In 1942, the Ministry of Home Security calculated that something like a million back garden 'Andersons' had been built throughout the country.

Although it was usually smelly and damp, and might even fill with water after heavy rain, the Anderson Shelter very successfully fulfilled its purpose, saving the lives of thousands of people throughout Britain. It also provided children with some of their best memories of the war. If you had a torch with batteries, you could wrap yourself in blankets and pass the time reading books and comics, or even doing your school homework. If the only faint light at night came from the candle under an up-turned flower pot that served as a heater – an ingenious device used in Anderson Shelters – then you could tell each other stories or listen to your mother or father telling you one. The stories of recently seen cinema films – which could be stretched out over several sessions, serial-form – passed the time in many air-raid shelters.

Not every family had an Anderson Shelter, even if they had space for one. The family of Mary Murphy, who was born in Chingford in Essex in 1939, did not have an Anderson Shelter. Her father, who had fought at Gallipoli in World War I, and then served as a special policeman in the City of London after 1939, had such terrible memories of helping dig out victims after air raids that he refused to even consider building one. He had no intention of letting himself and his family be buried alive.

Thus, when the V1 flying bombs, or 'doodlebugs', began their devastatingly indiscriminate attacks on southern England in 1944, five-year-old Mary found herself standing in the garden, her father holding her hand tightly as they watched the searchlights criss-crossing the night sky and listened to the sound of a doodlebug engine getting nearer and nearer, knowing that when the sound of the engine cut out she was to start counting to 50 during the eerie silence that followed. If she got to 50 before there was a loud explosion, that meant that the doodlebug had passed over them. 'I remember the fires after the doodlebugs exploded. Sometimes the whole horizon was ablaze,' Mary recalls.

Another very familiar air-raid shelter, also distributed free to low-income families, was the Morrison Shelter, named after Herbert Morrison, Minister of Home Security and later Home Secretary. This was designed for families without gardens, or for those people living in flats and other accommodation. This was a box-shaped shelter with a large and strong steel plate on top, which could be used as a table during the days and used as a double bed, or, if it had an inner shelf, as bunks for a family, at night. By November 1941 more than half a million Morrison Shelters had been made for use by families throughout Britain.

Mary Murphy's family did have a Morrison Shelter in their front room. During air raids, Mary got into the habit of retreating into the Morrison Shelter with her beaten-up teddy bear, her faithful golliwog and her tabby cat, John. The golliwog, a doll with a now totally unacceptable name, was a delightfully comfortable and huggable doll, and a favourite with small children in Britain until after the war. They were usually home-made, sometimes by mothers and sometimes by the children themselves. Even during the war, it was usually possible to find a pair of father's worn-out black socks, some rags to use as stuffing, a few strands of black and red wool, and a couple of buttons, which was all that was needed to make a golliwog.

The most famous of all Britain's air-raid shelters was the London Underground. At the height of the Blitz in September 1940, an estimated 177, 000 men, women and children were sheltering in Tube stations from the devastation being wrought above them. Although photographs show that many of the children who were taken down into Tube stations for the night took games, toys, books and even knitting with them, suggesting that the Underground played a big part in sheltering children during the war, in fact only about 9 per cent of the population used communal shelters. For most families, shelter from air raids was sought in Anderson and Morrison Shelters, in the cupboard under the stairs or even under the kitchen table: strong tables were much in demand during the war.

For families bombed out and left homeless after an air raid – which, in London after the end of the main Blitz in May 1941, meant one Londoner in every six – there was often a very long wait until something better than temporary accommodation in a shelter or a relative's home could be found. It was not until 1943 that the permanent repair of damaged houses, using good quality materials, could begin or the building of new homes get under way on any scale.

In the meantime, in the big cities, local

▶

4 November 1940: Children climbing into their bunks in an underground air raid shelter during the Blitz.

SURVIVING A BOMB IN A LONDON BOROUGH

'A very large bomb brought down hundreds of small houses [on a residential estate in Colwyn Street, Thamesborough]. The next morning the neighbourhood was a muddy wilderness of heaped rubble. Here and there [could be seen] the entrance to an Anderson Shelter, nearly buried under the debris... and quite a number of these little mud-covered igloos humping their backs out of the desolation. When the people crawled out in the morning they were covered in dust and mud... [But] the Andersons had done their work. Nearly eight hundred people were made homeless in Colwyn Street. Only three people were killed.' From *Front Line 1940–1941*, published for the Ministry of Home Security, 1942.

1940

MAY

15 Holland surrenders to Germany.

17 RAF raid on Germany.

20 German troops reach the Channel coast.

Auschwitz – Birkenau, the Nazi concentration camp, opens in Poland.

26 Evacuation of Allied troops from Dunkirk (Operation Dynamo) begins. Boys over the age of 15 rush to take part in the rescue attempts.

28 Belgium surrenders to Germany.

JUNE

3 The Luftwaffe bomb Paris for the first time.

4 Operation Dynamo ends, approximately 300,000 Allied troops have been evacuated from the shores of Dunkirk. Churchill makes his 'blood, toil, tears and sweat' speech.

5 The Battle of France begins.

10 Italy declares war on the United Kingdom and France.

Canada declares war on Italy.

Norway surrenders to Germany.

French government flees to Tours.

12 13,000 British and French troops surrender at St Valery-en-Caux.

authorities' social services, helped by volunteers, did what they could. In London's East End, the WVS evacuated children under five and the London County Council found billets for school-age children. Some local councils set up services so complicated that mothers, dealing with one official to get their children, some of school age and some younger, new ration books and identity cards, another one to get them all billets together, and yet another one if some, but not all, of her children were to be sent away, would give up in despair.

As the war dragged on, children found that, far more disturbing than long hours spent in shelters, days and nights hearing bombers flying overhead and bombs dropping, even the loss of their homes, was the absence of their parents. As conscription bit deeper, so more and more men were called up as age limits were extended. Even if one's father was not called up into the services, he could still be absent from his family because of his job, or because he spent many nights on ARP or fire-watching duties or in the Home Guard, which was not called 'Dad's Army' just because so many of its members were too old to fight in the services. It really was an army of fathers and grandfathers, brothers and uncles.

Many women were also absent from home much more than had ever been known in Britain. The needs of wartime industry took more and more women into essential wartime industries, or into a wide range of voluntary work, including the WVS, first-aid posts and much else. Even when she stayed at home, a mother might be occupied in some form of war work, including out work for munitions factories, which she and friends and neighbours could do at home, on the kitchen table.

While thousands of children were looked after by grandparents, often even being sent to live with them outside of the danger areas, for many more, charities and voluntary organisations had to fill child care gaps. Children were also helped by the increased provision of state-backed childcare facilities and the development of such things as British Restaurants, which allowed more and more women to work outside the home as the war went on. By 1944, 7 million of the 16 million British women aged between 14 and 59 had jobs in civil defence, industry or the armed forces.

Far worse for children than the absence from home of their parents was the death of one or both parents. Families with men fighting for their country lived in dread of the delivery of the telegram, often by a delivery boy who, at 14, was little more than a child himself, that told them their husband or son had been killed in action. Then there were the many children who survived an air raid that destroyed their home or shelter and left one or both parents and other members of their family dead.

When *Good Housekeeping* ran a story in the December 1944 issue called 'Nobody's Children' that looked at the problem of what to do in the long term with thousands of homeless children being looked after by such organisations as Dr Barnardo's Homes, which, at the time, was providing 25,000 meals a day for the 7,500 homeless children in its care, the response was enormous. Providing proper care for war orphans became an important part of the post-war Welfare State's programme, which built on the foundations laid by such war time organisations as the WVS working in

▲

Neighbours putting up Anderson Air Raid Shelters in their gardens during World War II.

1940

JUNE

14 The French government decamps to Bordeaux. Paris falls under German occupation.

16 Marshal Pétain becomes French Prime Minister. He immediately asks Germany for a peace deal.

17 German troops sink the troopship *Lancastria*.

18 Hitler and Mussolini meet in Munich.
Churchill announces that 'the Battle of France is over, the Battle of Britain is about to begin'.

22 France signs an armistice with Germany.

23 Hitler tours Paris.

24 France signs a formal surrender with Italy.

25 All hostilities cease on French soil.

30 German occupation of the Channel Islands begins.

JULY

1 Marshal Pétain establishes French government at Vichy.

5 French government breaks off relations with England.

10 The first phase of the Battle of Britain begins.

19 Hitler speaks at the Reichstag and urges Britain to see reason.
Denmark withdraws from the League of Nations.

23 Russia takes Lithuania, Latvia and Estonia.
Britain introduces a severe new form of taxation in the third 'war budget'.

tandem with charities like Barnardo's and service organisations like SSAFA (Soldiers, Sailors and Airmen's Families Association).

Other serious consequences for family life in Britain that resulted from the war were great rises in illegitimacy rates and in divorce, both a direct result of the widespread wartime attitude of 'live for today for tomorrow we may be dead'. There were thousands of quick marriages, with large numbers of girls marrying a man they had only known a week, in the few days before he was posted overseas. If he returned, often years later, the couple all too often would discover that they were strangers, with little in common.

With their husbands overseas for years at a time, many women had affairs that resulted in illegitimate babies. At the same time, a general loosening of attitudes towards morality led single women to be more relaxed about having sex outside marriage – in a period when contraception was less simple and easy to obtain, especially if a woman was single, than it became a couple of decades later. The result was an enormous increase in illegitimacy, so that by 1944 one in three births was illegitimate.

Despite such very sad and distressing problems, for the majority of the children of the war years life was surprisingly good. While it is true that the passing of time mellows memories, many adults who grew up during the war seem to have been not much disturbed by the actions of the enemy or by wartime deprivations. There was a certain excitement about living through extraordinary times coupled, for some, with a feeling that, since 'what will happen will happen', one may as well just get on with things.

As Patricia Houlahan, who spent the war in her family's

▶

September 1941: A son taking the place of his fighter pilot father pouring tea.

house in the naval city of Portsmouth, remembers, she and most of her friends were not much bothered by the day-to-day problems or aware of the horrors of war. '*We just got on with things. Even after whole nights spent in the Anderson shelter or next door in our neighbour's brick shelter, we* *always went off to school the next morning. Bombs and rockets did not bother me. The flares that the Germans dropped to guide their bombers to Portsmouth scared me much more. To this day, I cannot bear to listen to or look at fireworks.*'

DAILY LIFE IN WARTIME

*Two of the most important areas of children's daily life in wartime Britain –
how they were fed and how they were clothed – were both very quickly brought within
government rationing schemes. The government had had some experience of rationing
food during World War I, but what was planned now – and, indeed, had been planned for
some time – was something on a much bigger scale altogether.*

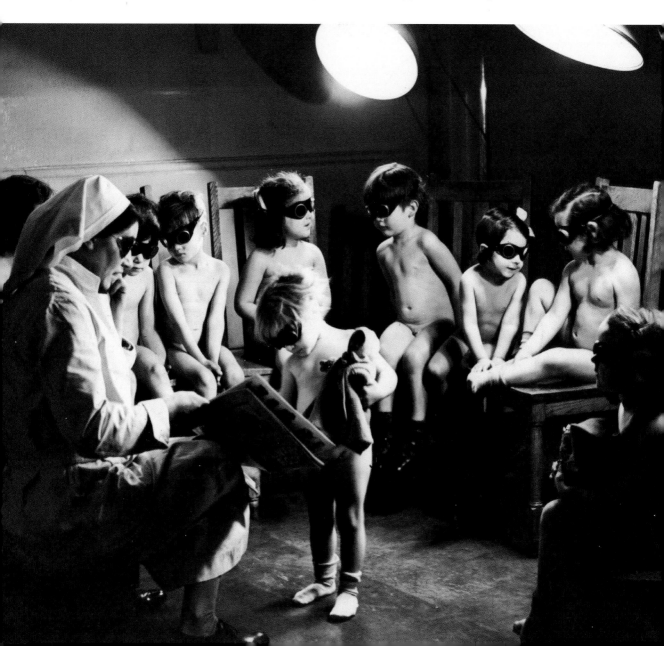

Statisticians and planners had long recognised that the availability and price of food was of national importance at all times as a symbol of the nation's well-being and prosperity. But in times of war it took on even greater significance: a country at war needed a well-fed and healthy population to keep wartime industries working at full capacity and to ensure that, once the war was over, there would be a generation of healthy, well-fed children to take over.

When ration books were first issued in January 1940, children under six (later reduced to under five) were given their own ration books, coloured green to distinguish them from the buff-coloured ration books of older children and adults. Children aged between 5 and 16 (later 18) also got their own ration books, coloured blue, from 1943. Expectant mothers were directed to obtain a child's green ration book from their local Food Office before their baby was born. Just as children were not exempt from having a National Registration Identity Card, so no child was exempt from having a ration book: the Imperial War Museum in London holds in its archives the ration book issued to Her Royal Highness Princess Elizabeth, of The Royal Lodge, Windsor Great Park, on 16 January 1940.

Ration books, which were brought in partly to prevent hoarding, were filled with coupons allocated to specific foods, allowed the Ministries of Food and Health to ensure that everyone got a fair share of foods, such as meat, dairy products, cooking fats, milk, sugar, preserves and eggs, that were regularly available. These foods were not rationed all at once in January 1940, but were added to the ration books over a period of 18 months or so. Fruit and vegetables were never rationed, but as fruit quickly became very scarce, with fruits from overseas, like oranges and bananas, being seldom seen, most children ate many more fresh vegetables than fresh fruits during the war.

◀

March 1942: A nurse watching over children in Bermondsey, London, sitting under sun-ray lamps to help make up the deficiency in sunlight and the lack of certain items of food, such as fruit, during the winter months.

1940

JULY

27 *A Wild Hare* is released, featuring Bugs Bunny.
29 Dover harbour is attacked by German bombers.

AUGUST

5 Hitler and Mussolini meet in Rome to discuss strategies after the defeat of France.
8 Heavy air battles over the Channel.
11 Battle of Britain begins in earnest.
13 German bombing offensive against airfields and factories in Britain.
17 Hitler announces total blockade of the British Isles.
20 Churchill pays tribute to the Royal Air Force.
23 First German air raids on Central London.
25 First British air raid on Berlin.
31 RAF Fighter Command lose 38 planes in Luftwaffe attacks on their HQ.

SEPTEMBER

7 The Blitz begins. Nazi bombs rain down on London. This is the first of 57 consecutive nights of bombing in the capital. During the onslaught two million houses are destroyed and approximately 32,000 civilians are killed.

A high point of the war for many children came in July 1942 when a 'personal points' scheme covering chocolate and sweets came in. Now everyone over the age of six months could buy, or have bought for them, 8oz (250g) of chocolate and confectionary every month without using up precious food coupons. Chocolate bars, rather smaller than before the war and often wrapped in greaseproof paper to save precious tinfoil, became a regular item in many children's shopping baskets, despite the fact that the chocolate was powdery and not as smooth as it had been and was also, much of it, dark because of the shortage of milk.

Beside chocolate bars there might also be in a child's shopping basket paper bags, or screws of paper (if just a pennyworth was purchased) containing such delights as acid drops, fruit drops, bulls' eyes, humbugs, liquorice comforts and many other sweets. After a time the chocolate and sweet ration went up to 16oz (500g) before dropping back to 12oz (375g), where it remained until sweet rationing finally ended in 1953, eight years after the war ended.

Children, except those under five, who got half the meat ration and orange juice instead of tea, were allowed the same ration quantities as adults. Another concession for small children was being allowed three eggs a week; they also got double the allowance of dried eggs as adults when these were introduced. A points system, brought in later, gave everyone 16 points a month which could be spent as one chose on a range of foods covered by the points rather than by the coupons in ration books, including tins of corned beef, spam, and pulses like split peas or dried beans.

Mothers, clutching their children's ration books as well as their own, and possibly with one or two small children with them, would use much of the time spent standing in queues outside shops deciding which of the several books in their shopping bags would have its meat coupons removed and which would be used for butter, eggs or sugar. They might get their children to carry the sheets of newspaper that many of them took to the shops for wrapping up their purchases.

Children's health and nutrition were major priorities during the war. As well as providing free immunisation against such childhood diseases as diphtheria, the government also developed several schemes aimed at ensuring children's nutritional needs were met. Among them were the National Milk Scheme and the Vitamin

A VERY IMPORTANT NUMBER

Identity cards, which everyone, young and old, was issued with at the beginning of the war and had to carry at all times, so that it could be produced when someone in authority asked to see it, had a personal number, unique to the card's carrier. The National Registration Number was also used on such things as ration books, so it is not surprising that many people can still, at the beginning of the 21st century, reel off their wartime Identity Card number without a second's hesitation. Jane Elliott, given her Identity Card when she was a pupil of Harrogate Ladies College, remembers that its number was KIAB 413, while that of Martin Wagrel, at school in Aberdeen, was SUFD 203.

Three young children enjoying a portable, healthy snack – a carrot on a stick. Ice cream is not available due to war rationing.

Welfare Scheme, while the creation of the long, grey-looking but undeniably very nutritious National Loaf and Household Milk – dried milk powder that was turned into milk by mixing the powder with water – benefited children as much as adults.

The National Milk Scheme was a development of a scheme begun in the 1930s to get milk to children from the poorest families. The wartime scheme, begun in 1940, was by 1944 getting free milk to 19 out of every 20 children entitled to it. The pre-war schoolchildren's free or subsidised milk scheme was also continued and extended so that something like three-quarters of state schoolchildren were getting a third of a pint of subsidised, very nutritious milk in school every day.

Not every schoolchild liked his or her school milk, of course. To begin with, it was room temperature, if not actually warm, and there was often dust on the cardboard top because the crates of milk had been sitting in a school corridor or outside in the

▲

December 1940: A row of toddlers, evacuated from London during the Blitz, have their feet inspected at their new home in a 15th-century mansion house in Kent.

playground. But it was easy enough to blow the dust off, push in the central button on the top with the end of your straw, and then drink the milk. And if you were permitted to drink it in class, it made a break from lessons.

The Ministry of Food considered that providing infants and young children with vitamin foods was so important that coupons for vitamin foods, including orange juice and cod liver oil, were included in a revised children's ration book, called the R.B.2. As well as this, the Vitamin Welfare Scheme was begun in December 1941 as a follow-up to an earlier scheme aimed at countering vitamin deficiency in infants by issuing free blackcurrant juice and cod liver oil. The blackcurrant juice was eventually replaced by concentrated orange juice, much of which came from the United States as part of the lend–lease scheme.

The Ministry of Food did its best to inform mothers of where they could get the orange juice and cod liver oil to which they were entitled. But bureaucracy, as ever, got in the way, making mothers apply first to a Food Office,

DRIED EGGS: A WARTIME BAD MEMORY

Among many children's worst wartime food memories are powdery scrambled eggs and puddings 'looking like linoleum tiles' that were made from dried egg powder. Available on the ration as one packet (the equivalent of a dozen eggs) per person every four weeks, dried egg powder was a substitute for scarce fresh eggs, with the earliest to appear coming from America. To reconstitute the dried egg to make the equivalent of one fresh egg, One level tablespoon of the powder had to be mixed with two tablespoons of water. If a mother optimistically added too much powder to the water she achieved an egg with a rather unpleasant taste – as many wartime children still remember. Despite the Ministry of Food's many recipes and detailed advice for using the dried egg powder, it was never used with any enthusiasm.

1940

SEPTEMBER

12 In France 17,000-year-old Lascaux cave paintings are discovered by a group of young Frenchmen on a hiking trip.

26 The US places a total embargo on the shipping of scrap metals to Japan.

27 Germany, Italy and Japan sign the Tripartite Pact.

OCTOBER

4 Hitler and Mussolini meet in an armoured train at the Brenner Pass to discuss war progress.

9 Winston Churchill is elected leader of the Conservative Party.

28 Italy invades Greece.

NOVEMBER

3 First British troops arrive in Greece.

5 Roosevelt is elected President of the USA for a third term.
Armed merchant cruiser *Jervis Bay* is sunk by battleship *Admiral Scheer* in the Atlantic.

12 Soviet foreign minister Vyacheslav Molotov arrives in Berlin for talks with Hitler.

13 Walt Disney's *Fantasia* is released – his first box-office failure.

14 German bombs decimate the city of Coventry.

1940

NOVEMBER

19 Birmingham is attacked by Luftwaffe bombers for over nine hours.

20 Hungary agrees to join the Axis powers.

22 Greeks defeat the Italian 9th Army.

23 Romania joins Axis alliance.

24 Slovakia joins the Tripartite Pact.

26 The Jewish ghetto in Warsaw is sealed off from the rest of the city.

DECEMBER

2 The Luftwaffe carry out night raids on Bristol.

5 Hitler lays out plans to invade Russia.

7 The RAF carry out a night raid on Düsseldorf.

9 Operation Compass. The British begin a western desert offensive in North Africa against the Italians.

12 Over 20,000 Italians are taken prisoner during Operation Compass.

13 German troops move into Romania from Hungary.

22 Aircraft from the HMS *Illustrious* bomb Tripoli.

26 After a brief Christmas respite the Germans resume their bombing of London.

29/30 Massive German air-raid on London.

31 British casualties for the month of December are 3,793 killed and 5,244 injured.

which might be in another town, for their free coupons and then sending them somewhere else, such as a welfare centre, clinic or distribution centre, to get them. Many mothers never availed themselves of the scheme and three-quarters of the cod liver oil made available by the Ministry was not used. The unpleasant taste of cod liver oil did not help, of course, and many mothers preferred to give it to their children in the form of a spoonful of the much more pleasant malt extract with added cod liver oil and orange juice.

By the time the war ended in 1945, one child in three was getting a meal, free or subsidised (at a cost to parents of just four or five pence, the price of a child's ticket at the cinema), at school. For many of these children, the school meal, often including vegetables grown in the school's own allotment, was the most nutritious of the day. For those schools that did not have their own canteen, the nearest British Restaurant – another very successful scheme to get cheap, nutritious and off-ration food to people in wartime – made an excellent substitute.

For children at boarding schools mealtimes left mixed memories. Kenneth Jones, at school in Devon, does not remember ever being bothered by the rationing. *'Every Monday morning we were issued with our personal ration of sugar and butter. There was always a lot of bartering in accordance with our personal tastes – "I will swap half my sugar for half your butter". Then, one day a week we would spend the afternoon helping local farmers and were given a smashing tea with Devonshire clotted cream, strawberries, home-baked buns etc. We boys certainly didn't suffer, at least during the early years of the war.'*

▶

Children say a prayer before a meal at a crèche which was formed to enable factory working mothers to leave their children safely during daytime.

1944: Piccadilly tube station, London, being used as an air raid shelter during the night.

Joan Elliott, whose school was evacuated from Harrogate to the imposing Swinton Castle on the Yorkshire moors, remembers the grandeur of her surroundings, but also being hungry and, in the cold of winter, getting chilblains. The thought of the tins of water biscuits back at home in the cellar air-raid shelter was often tantalising. It was a Red Letter Day when Lady Swinton, whom she encountered in a lift in the castle, offered her a peppermint.

YES, WE HAVE NO BANANAS

Bananas were so seldom seen in Britain during the war that not only was a song about the lack of them very popular in East End community singalongs, but many children, like little Annabel Rudland in Stevenage, who was six when the war ended, remember when the first bananas arrived from the West Indies when the war was over. Probably Annabel, like many others, had not been deceived by a wartime children's pudding which, although called 'Mashed Bananas', had actually consisted of cooked parsnips and pieces of the grey National Loaf mashed up with a little sugar and a few drops of banana essence. Annabel, being too young, would have missed out on the time when, a full consignment of bananas having made it safely to Britain, the Ministry of Food decided that a 'special ration' of one banana should be given to every child over 14.

POPULAR CULTURE IN 1941

Popular Songs

Chattanooga Choo Choo, by Glenn Miller
A String of Pearls, by Glenn Miller
Green Eyes, by Jimmy Dorsey
Amapola (Pretty Little Poppy) by Jimmy Dorsey
God Bless the Child, by Billie Holiday
Boogie Woogie Bugle Boy, by the Andrews Sisters

High-grossing films

Sergeant York, starring Gary Cooper
Buck Privates , starring Abbott and Costello
Tobacco Road, starring Charley Grapewin
Dumbo, Walt Disney animation
How Green Was My Valley, starring Walter Pidgeon and Maureen O'Hara.

JANUARY

Rationing of clothes introduced in Britain.

8 Robert Baden-Powell, the founder of Scouting, dies.

10 HMS *Illustrious* is hit by Axis aircraft while in a convoy on its way to Malta.

29 British advance into Italian Somaliland from Kenya. Anglo American talks begin on the consequences of US entry into the war.

While trying to ensure that their children were adequately fed remained a constant worry for mothers, keeping them well clothed soon began to worry them almost as much. They were still wrestling with the problems of food ration books, coupons and points when the government introduced clothes rationing in June 1941. Now every man, woman and child in the country had another ration book, again with one's identity card number on the front, to deal with.

The basic clothes ration was 66 coupons (later in the war reduced to 60) per person per year, except in the first year of clothes rationing, when the coupons had to last 15 months. When it was realised that the purchase of a new winter coat would mean handing over 13 coupons along with payment, while a pair of men's trousers took eight coupons and a dress 11, mothers knew that new clothing was not going to figure regularly in their children's lives. It was all very well for *Good Housekeeping* magazine to tell mother that she could buy a delightful 'Buster Utility suit', including a shirt and lined trousers, for her little boy for just ten shillings and twopence, plus four clothing coupons, for reality did not always match up with the optimistic tone women's magazines tried their best to convey during the war. More than one wartime child still remembers the annoyance of having to give up clothing coupons so that an older brother or sister, now old enough to leave school and take on a job, could buy new trousers or a coat to go to work in.

On the other hand, recalling the ingenuity with which they and their mothers 'made do and mended', provides many an amusing memory. Just as well as she remembers the arrival of the first banana in her home, Annabel Rudland remembers the excitement of going to the nearby Henlow RAF base with her mother to buy used parachute silk for making into nightgowns and underwear.

For other girls the memories centre on learning to knit. Although new wool became increasingly hard to buy and was rationed anyway, with one clothing coupon being needed to buy one 2oz (50g) ball, there were always many old jumpers that one's brothers and sisters had grown out of that could be carefully washed, unravelled and knitted up again into something with an entirely new, although rather curly and wrinkled, look. This reuse of odd bits of wool accounted for the wonderfully striped jumpers, cardigans, gloves and hats worn by many children – and their mothers – during the war.

When the Utility Clothing scheme was adopted in 1941, children's clothes were included in it. Because the scheme was devised by the government to control both the amount of precious raw materials used in the manufacture of clothing and the amount of the finished fabrics put into garments, everyone assumed the clothes would be unattractive. In fact, because ten leading designers, including Queen Elizabeth's dressmakers Norman Hartnell and Hardy Amies, were involved in the design of the clothes, they turned out to be both well-designed and of good quality. Where girls, with their natural liking for ribbons, buttons and bows, may have felt they were losing out was in the introduction of something called Austerity regulations. These drastically limited the amount of frills and decorations that could be put on clothes, both adults' and children's.

For most people, buying new clothes, whether Utility or Austerity, rationed or not, played a very small part in daily life. A much bigger role was played by the business of making do with what clothing you had and mending it – again and again and again. 'Make do and Mend' was another slogan, like 'Dig for Victory', dreamed up by the propaganda men and women of the Ministry of Information (MoI) for the Board of Trade, the government department responsible for clothing, in an effort to make shabbiness not just acceptable, but a patriotic duty.

▶

27 February 1943: Only a limited range of children's clothing is available during the period of rationing.

1941

FEBRUARY

3 German forces restore Pierre Laval to office in Vichy, France.

9 In a radio broadcast Winston Churchill pleads with the US to show its support for the Allied troops by sending arms.

11 British forces advance into Italian Somaliland in East Africa.
The Luftwaffe sink five British merchant ships off the Azores.

12 German General Erwin Rommel arrives in Tripoli, North Africa.

14 First units of German 'Afrika Korps' arrive in North Africa.

19/ The town of Swansea in
22 South Wales is obliterated during three nights of intensive bombing. 230 people are killed.

MARCH

Captain America comics issues its first *Captain America & Bucky* comic.

1 Bulgaria joins Axis powers.

2 Germany occupies Bulgaria.

7 British forces arrive in Greece.

11 President Roosevelt signs the Lend-Lease Arms Bill which officially becomes law in the USA.

17 British Minister of Labour, Ernest Bevin, calls for women to fill vital jobs.

▲

12 August 1940: Children gardening during their holidays at a school in Cobham, Surrey.

▶

3 December 1941: Young patients sitting on their mothers' laps at Miss Dane's clinic in Lewisham, London. The clinic treats children traumatised by bombs during World War II.

Again like the 'Dig for Victory' campaign, children were as much a target of the 'Make do and Mend' campaign as their parents, with many leaflets and posters from the Board of Trade being aimed specifically at children. 'Useful jobs that girls can do – to help win the war' and 'Simple jobs boys can do themselves – and so help win the war' were the headlines on two.

The poster aimed at boys gave quite detailed instructions on how to mend a table leg or do simple electrical repairs, but also, in a departure from the norm, on how to sew on a button or darn a sock. The girls' poster, while concentrating on the business of making, repairing and looking after clothes, also threw in instructions on how to refix a loose knife handle or sort out a sticking drawer. Looking after clothes was a theme carried on in many girls' schools, with instructresses coming in from outside to advise girls on how they could make their school clothes and uniforms last longer by being let out, patched and added to so that they would continue to fit growing girls.

Children in the German-occupied Channel Islands would have envied their mainland counterparts their reasonably available, even if rationed, food and their clothing, however limited in quantity. Rationing, curfews and censorship of books and newspapers were all imposed on the Islanders from the beginning of the Occupation.

As the war went on and Hitler decided to turn the Channel Islands into an 'Atlantic Wall', things got very much worse. The staple diet was reduced to root vegetables, while blackberry, rose leaves and dock weeds were used to make 'tea'. While British mothers – although perhaps not their children – were irritated when soap rationing was imposed without warning in February 1942, at least they had enough to keep their families and their homes and clothes clean. Soap was in such short supply in the Channel Islands that the smallest cut on unwashed skin would fester and leg sores, dubbed 'Occupation ulcers' by one doctor, were common.

GOING TO SCHOOL
IN WARTIME

The education system was turned upside down when war broke out.
There was chaos and confusion for weeks after the evacuation scheme for schools
was put into action on 1 September 1939, the day on which it had been planned to
coincide a return to school after the summer holidays with the raising of the
school-leaving age from 14 to 15, which now did not happen for another eight years.

Thus, many 14-year-olds who, in peacetime, would have had another year's schooling, found themselves being treated as young adults in a nation at war, able not only to get themselves paid jobs, but also to help with Civil Defence work, including fire-fighting, auxiliary nursing, ARP work and much else.

Under the schools evacuation scheme, schools in the Reception Areas could, if necessary, operate a shift system, usually two shifts a day, but occasionally three, so that an evacuated school could share the premises with the local school. This system was in operation, more or less successfully, by the middle of September, although in both the Reception and the Neutral Areas, the re-opening of many schools was delayed by the need to complete the provision of shelters, which all schools were required to have. If the school grounds allowed it, shelters were dug in the playground, but many schools had to use inner corridors without windows as their main shelters. In some very small, usually primary schools, no shelters could be provided, and children regularly practised running home as quickly as possible in the event of an air raid warning – which, since these were in areas hopefully far from air raids, ought not to be very often, if at all.

There were, not surprisingly, many problems to be overcome in integrating large groups of children from the industrial cities into schools in quiet towns and villages far from urban life. It was all very well for children used to having their school to themselves, with desks for everyone, to be told, when being shunted about to make room for the newcomers, that 'There's a war on, you know, we must all make adjustments'. Differences in dress, behaviour, accent and language were swiftly noted and led, if not to a ganging-up in the playground, then certainly to a tendency for the newcomers to gather together in a self-protecting group. There were many playground fights during those difficult weeks of evacuation, and not always between the local children and the newcomers: sometimes the fighting would be between boys from different parts of London's East End.

In the Evacuation Areas, in theory now without schoolchildren and schoolteachers, as many as 2,000 state elementary and secondary schools (which were a mixture of technical schools and grammar schools) were taken over by the Civil Defence services and put to use as shelters for those left homeless

A group of young evacuees in Monmouthshire, Wales find plenty to help alleviate their homesickness during World War II. Some have never seen a climbing frame before, such as this one situated in a local playground.

1941

MARCH

24 British Somaliland is cleared of Italians, but Rommel reoccupies El Agheila.

25 Yugoslavia signs the Tripartite Act.

27 A coup in Yugoslavia overthrows the pro-Axis government and King Peter takes control.
Second phase of Battle of Keren in Eritrea ends in British victory.

30 Axis make counter-offensive moves in Cyrenaica, North Africa, with the help of the German 5th Light Division under Rommel.

31 British cruisers HMS *York* and HMS *Bonaventure* are sunk by the Italians in a period of five days.

APRIL

3 Germany marches into Hungary.

6 Germany invades Greece and Yugoslavia.
Allied forces enter Addis Ababa.

7 British promise allegiance to Yugoslavia.

9 Germans enter Thessaloniki and Rommel takes Bardia.

10 Germans enter Zagreb.
Hungary invades Yugoslavia.
Croatia made an independent state.

by bombing, as storage areas, ARP posts, first-aid posts and other things. As many families did not send their children out of the Evacuation Areas, there were soon many thousands of children running wild and unsupervised in Britain's cities. To these numbers were gradually added hundreds more as evacuated mothers and children began to drift back to the cities. Many of these children got what education they could by joining home tuition classes organised in private houses, in pubs and in other

A LOGISTICAL NIGHTMARE

The problems encountered by the education authorities of the London outer suburb of Croydon in keeping track of their school-age children were typical of those experienced by many local education authorities. According to a post-war report undertaken by Croydon Corporation, there were more than 20,000 school pupils in Croydon in 1939, most of them in elementary schools, where five out of six children in England and Wales spent all their school lives. In the weeks and months after evacuation, schools and their teachers were scattered from one end of England – Penzance in Cornwall – to the other – Newcastle-upon-Tyne. Once in the 110 different places to which they were sent, weeks went by before many teachers found permanent places to set up their classrooms. Teachers were reduced to arranging a regular meeting point every day, from which their pupils would be marched off to whatever place was available to house them that day.

distinctly non-educational surroundings.

Although the government acknowledged the inevitable at the beginning of November 1939 and permitted the reopening of state schools in the Evacuation Areas, where parents wanted them, it was not until mid-1941, more than a year after the Board of Education had reintroduced compulsory education, that enough schools had re-opened to get all children off the street, and back into full-time education. A major reason for delays in opening was the time it took to sort out the details of shelter construction, including how strong they should be and who, whether the local authority or the Board of Education, would pay for them. For many children in Britain's most deprived areas, there was a very long period without the free milk and free meals (to which they were entitled) in schools. As for the scabies, head lice and other parasites that had so shocked the nation in 1939, these went virtually untreated in many working-class elementary schools until the middle of 1941, when school medical inspections got back to their pre-war frequency.

Many independent or public schools, which educated only one schoolchild in every ten in England and Wales in 1939, evacuated themselves to the country, many of them to large country houses and stately homes. Perhaps the most important public school evacuation of the war was that of the famous Worcestershire boys' school,

◄

13 September 1941: Boys from the St John's School in Redhill, Surrey have a lesson in the school air raid shelter. The historical murals on the walls were all painted by pupils.

1941

APRIL

12 Belgrade surrenders.

13 Russia and Japan sign five-year neutrality agreement.

14 Rommel attacks Tobruk.

17 Yugoslavia surrenders to the Germans, the RAF evacuate King Peter.

19 Germany attacks Greece. Empire troops land in Iraq.

21 British troops asked to withdraw from Greece.

27 Greece surrenders to the Germans.
Axis forces cross Egyptian frontier as they progress eastwards.

MAY

Breakfast cereal Cheerios is introduced as CheeriOats by General Mills.
Orson Welles' film *Citizen Kane* premieres in New York City.

1 German attack on Tobruk is repulsed.

2 Iraqis attack British in Habbaniya.

5 Emperor Haile Selassie returns to his throne in triumph.

6 British triumphant over defeat of Iraqi forces.

10 Deputy Führer Rudolph Hess parachutes into Scotland, apparently on a peace mission.

Malvern College, to Blenheim Palace, birthplace of Winston Churchill, who replaced Neville Chamberlain as Prime Minister in May 1940. While the boys of Malvern College found themselves in classrooms and dormitories hung with famous paintings and valuable tapestries depicting the military successes of Churchill's famous ancestor, the 1st Duke of Marlborough, their old college was taken over by the government's Telecommunications (or radar) Research Establishment in May 1942. Where there was some truth in the saying that the Battle of Waterloo had been won on the playing fields of Eton, there was even more in the quip that World War II was won on the playing fields of Malvern College – especially the junior boys' playing fields, which soon disappeared under experiments involving the ground radar devices that did more than anything else to give victory, especially in the air, to Britain and her Allies.

Double-shift education was first experienced in Britain, because of a shortage of teachers, during World War I. It had been something of an educational disaster, and the teaching profession was anxious to avoid the same thing happening after 1939. Trying to ensure that full-time schooling continued led to many shifts and stratagems, from holding classes out-of-doors in parks and fields in fine weather – fortunately, September 1939 was a very fine summer – to taking over any suitably big enough building or large room in buildings. Church halls, village halls, large rooms in public houses and even theatres and cinemas were all turned over to the business of educating the nation's children.

▶

A group of evacuees having an open-air maths lesson in a hayfield near a village in Monmouthshire, Wales, 14 June 1940.

HOW TO BE A TEACHER

At the outbreak of war, there were two main kinds of teacher in English state schools: qualified and unqualified. Qualified teachers were those who had completed courses at teacher training colleges. Unqualified teachers were teachers who had not gone to a training college, perhaps staying on as unqualified teachers at the school where they had finished their schooldays as pupil-teachers. It was possible for unqualified teachers, especially in more remote village schools, to pass all their learning and working lives in the one school. As the war went on, a third category of teacher began to appear in elementary schools. These were 'supplementary teachers', who needed only to be over the age of 18 and to have been vaccinated to qualify to help teach the nation's children.

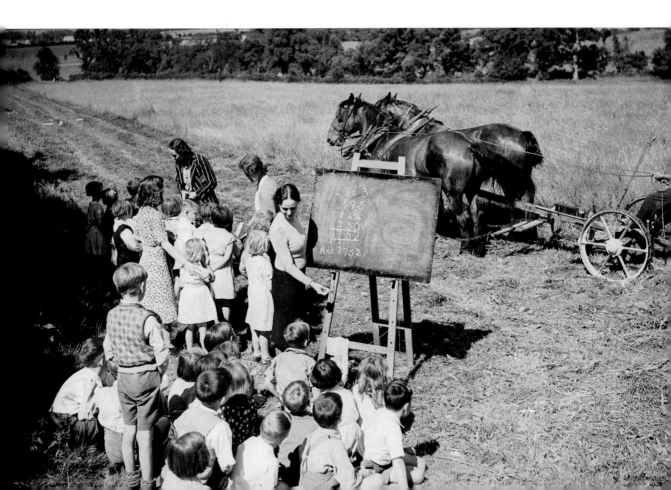

As with other aspects of life in Britain, there had long been a marked difference between the standards of teaching and the facilities available in middle-class state schools and those available in schools in poorer, working-class and inner-city areas. It was a difference exacerbated by the war. While the obvious problems and deficiencies of state school education in Britain had become of increasing concern to the government throughout the 1930s, the children of the war years also had to grapple with many serious practical problems.

As more and more young male teachers were called up into the armed services, the lack of qualified teachers became a problem. Many people, recalling their wartime schooldays, have vivid memories of the increasing age and female gender of their teachers. Some schools ended the war with all-female teaching staffs, many of whom were married – something not permitted before the war – and many more of whom were well past retirement age and therefore trained in an earlier age. Children began to experience the sort of teaching, involving much chanting of arithmetic tables and the rules of spelling, that their grandparents had known. In secondary or 'selective' schools where subjects like Classics were still on the timetable, vicars who had never taught in their lives found themselves trying, often without much success, to keep order in increasingly large classes instead of instilling the rudiments of Latin and Greek into their pupils.

Almost as difficult for Britain's state school children as the lack of well-qualified teachers was the lack of all kinds of teaching equipment, including such basic materials as pens, pencils and paper. Paper was in short supply, and bits of paper of every kind were hoarded carefully. Many children used newspaper for painting on during art lessons, and squared-up bits of paper on which to practise their cross-stitch and other embroidery stitches. Wartime economy paper in exercise books was full of woodchips, and the exercise books themselves were in such short supply that children had to use them very carefully. Some schools resorted to guillotining exercise books in half, so that every child in a class had some sort of book in which to write.

Then, there were the poor quality pencils. Made out of cedar wood – unpainted because to give them a smooth, colourful coating would be to waste paint – their lead was thin and broke easily. Some schools cut pencils in half as well as exercise books, and many teachers gathered up the pencils at the end of lessons and put them away carefully. Fountain pens were also in short supply, so most children wrote with dip pens, dipping

◀

Peter Neve having a gas mask fitted on by his teacher during drill at school.

the nibs into inkwells filled with inferior ink, which it was the responsibility of the class's ink monitor to mix up from a powder. Indian ink, always very scarce, often disappeared altogether from the classroom.

But worse than the lack of basic materials was the absence of textbooks from the classroom. From the infant classes' readers to the texts of Shakespeare's plays needed by pupils anxious to pass their School Certificate and Higher School Certificate exams, textbooks became increasingly difficult to replace as the war went on. Of course, for many older children, exams in wartime took on a special, not necessarily all bad flavour. There was the thrill of being able to write on your exam paper that your exam had been 'interrupted by an air raid warning for one hour and 40 minutes', while the interruption itself, during which you had very carefully not talked to your fellow pupils in the shelter and certainly not discussed the paper with anyone, at least allowed you to marshal a few facts in your head.

Many older schoolchildren 'doing their bit for the war effort', found that exams got in the way. Joining an ARP team, being in the Girl Guides or Boy Scouts, perhaps helping with a Cubs group or helping in your local hospital one night a week left little time for revising for exams. Many men and women, recalling their war-time schooldays, think that they only passed their School Certificate because the examiners were extra kind.

Many schools put a lot of time into the 'war effort', both in school and outside. School assemblies gave head teachers a chance to keep their pupils up to date with the course of the war and to read out letters sent from the war zones by former teachers and pupils. Some children would say years later that the only geography they were taught in school during the war involved studying maps of the various parts of the world where British troops were fighting. There was a lot of practical help, too. Many schools sponsored particular parts of the armed services, with naval vessels being popular. Girls, following the lead of Princess Elizabeth and Princess Margaret, who were photographed knitting socks for servicemen, might knit balaclavas, thick socks and mittens for sailors on the Arctic convoys and pupils would write letters to crew members. For schools in country areas, the 'war effort' was more likely to consist of helping the 'Dig for Victory' campaign by taking half-days out of school to help local farmers with the harvest.

SCHOOLS AND THE NIGHT AIR RAIDS

As with most things, schools in the bombing areas soon devised a rule covering absence from school in the event of a night-time air raid. If the all-clear sounded before midnight, children were expected to be in school before 8.45 the next morning, no matter how many hours they had spent in the Anderson shelter or in the cupboard under the stairs. Only if the all-clear had sounded after midnight could children come into school in late morning, in time for their school dinner. In London, children who spent their nights in an Underground station were assumed to have had a reasonable night's sleep – which, perhaps after many nights of practice, they did. In a good few cases, of course, there was no school to return to after an air raid. One in five of the nation's schools was badly damaged by bombs during the war.

17 April 1942: Schoolchildren line up to pay at their classroom post office, where they raise money during Warship Week.

1941
MAY

16 Final British reinforcements arrive in Crete.

18 New German warships *Bismarck* and *Prinz Eugen* sail into the Baltic Sea.

19 Germans sink the Egyptian liner *Zamzam* carrying 200 Americans, in the South Atlantic.

22-23 Heavy German air attacks on Crete sink cruisers *Fiji* and *Gloucester* and destroyer *Greyhound*. Luftwaffe sinks two more British destroyers *Kashmir* and *Kelly*.

24 *Bismarck* sinks the British ship *Hood*.
Heavy German bombing of Crete and King of Greece leaves for Cairo.

25 *Bismarck* escapes Royal Navy pursuit.

27 British Navy sink the *Bismarck* 400 miles (640 km) west of Brest.
Germans take Canea in Crete and British withdraw from the island.
President Roosevelt proclaims an 'unlimited national emergency'.

28 Allied forces evacuate from Heraklion in Crete.
Roosevelt says that the Neutrality Act needs to be repealed.

29 Over 200 men killed when the destroyer *Orion* is attacked off Crete – two destroyers are lost.

▲

1941: Children at their lessons in an air raid shelter during World War II.

▶

1940: A 'roving teacher' holds a class in the living room of a house in Beckenham, Kent, during World War II. Many homes have been turned into temporary classrooms while local schools are shut due to bombing, so that the children are never more than two minutes from home.

This positive, patriotic approach to the war no doubt helped many schoolchildren safely and confidently through their schooling, which may not have included such frills as cookery lessons or outdoor sports, but in most cases gave them a good grounding in the three 'Rs'. But there is no denying that many children were deprived of a decent education during World War II and ended up, if not totally illiterate, then certainly very educationally below standard. National Conscription, brought in for men at the beginning of the war, did not end until the late 1950s, by which time it was clear that far too many young men called up into the post-war services had a poor grasp of basic skills such as reading, writing and simple maths.

Luckily things started to improve with the reformation of education in England and Wales signalled by the Education Act of 1944 which began to show positive results. R. A. Butler, who was President of the Board of Education for much of the war, steered through Parliament the Education Act of 1944 that led the way to a comprehensive reformation of the education system in England and Wales (but not Scotland, which had its own education system).

THE BUTLER EDUCATION ACT

As well as raising the school leaving age to 15, which the post-war Labour government put into effect in 1947, the Education Act of 1944 reorganised secondary education in England and Wales. The elementary schools that had been the only school experienced by the majority of children were replaced at secondary level – that is, at age '11 plus' – by a tripartite system that, it was hoped, would allow a more democratic 'parity of esteem' among schoolchildren. The Act provided for grammar schools for the more academically able children, technical schools for those with a more technically minded bent, and secondary moderns for those children not comfortable in either of the first two categories. In practice, things did not work out quite as R. A. Butler and his Board had hoped. During the 1940s and 1950s, local authorities built few technical schools and the majority of children were educated in secondary modern schools, some of which demonstrated very low expectations indeed of their pupils.

◀

15 September 1941: A couple of toddlers grooming themselves in front of a mirror in the garden of the Muriel Green Nursery Centre, in St Albans, where women war workers can send their babies to be looked after during the day.

1941
JUNE

1 17,000 Allied troops are successfully evacuated from Crete.

2 Ruhr industrial area bombed by the RAF.

4 The ex-Kaiser of Germany Wilhelm II dies in exile at Doorn, Netherlands.

7 First of five night raids on Brest by the RAF.

8 Allies invade Syria and Lebanon.

9 British advance 40 miles (64 kilometres) into southern Syria and Lebanon. Occupation of Tyre.

11 RAF raids Rhr, Rhineland and German ports in the first of 20 consecutive night raids.

14 President Roosevelt orders that all German and Italian assets in the USA are to be frozen.

16 Roosevelt orders the closure of all German consulates on US territory.

19 Germany and Italy expel US consul officials in retaliation for US moves.

21 Allied troops occupy Damascus.

22 Germany attacks Russia as Operation Barbarossa begins. Greatest military offensive in the history of the war.
Italy and Romania declare war on Russia.

23 Hungary and Slovakia declare war on the Soviet Union.

24 Germans capture Vilna and Kaunas as they move east into Russia.

HELPING THE
WAR EFFORT

*World War II was like no other war that Britain had been involved in.
Because it was fought on the Home Front as well as in many far away countries,
there was no way that children could be kept sheltered in happy ignorance of the fact
that there was a war on. From the beginning, the government reached out to children
old enough to help in war work.*

Once the great evacuation of mothers and children from the perceived war zones had been completed – and the planning for this had closely involved the children for months before it actually took place – various ministries quickly swung into action with such famous schemes as the 'Dig for Victory' and 'Make do and Mend' campaigns.

The DIG FOR VICTORY campaign – to use the capital letters in which the government launched its great scheme at the outbreak of war – was essential to the country's survival because much agricultural land had been given over to pasture or taken out of use as the country's reliance on food imports increased in the 1930s. German U-boats in the Atlantic greatly diminished the amount of food Britain could expect to receive from the countries in the Empire. The 'Dig for Victory' campaign was therefore conducted on a very large scale indeed, with millions of propaganda posters and instructional leaflets being distributed the length and breadth of the country.

Although when he launched the 'Dig for Victory' scheme in a BBC broadcast in October 1939, the Agriculture Minister, Sir Reginald Dorman-Smith, called only on men and women to dig an allotment in their spare time, his words won an enthusiastic response from children, too, which the government was not slow to respond to. Among the hundreds of brightly coloured 'Dig for Victory' posters that began pouring out of the Ministry of Food, many actually showed children doing the digging and the Ministry reinforced the message by distributing posters and leaflets to schools in every part of the country to be pinned up in classrooms, canteens and corridors.

◀

3 August 1942: The Duke of Norfolk demonstrates the correct way to hold a rabbit during an exhibition designed to educate people about growing their own food.

1941

JUNE

26 Finland declares war on Russia.
Heavy fighting in Minsk as the Germans continue to advance.
27 Hungary declares war on USSR.
28 Germans capture Minsk. Albania declares war on the Soviet Union.
29 Göring is named as Hitler's successor.
30 Germans advance in Russian-occupied Poland, taking control of Lvov.
It was also during the month of June 1941 that the Nazi SS Einsatgrüppen began their mass murder.

JULY

1 Daylight offensives by RAF begin over Northern France, Channel and Occupied Europe.
2 Japan calls up 1 million men for military service.
8 Soviet President Litninov broadcasts from Moscow in English, stating that the UK and Russia must stand up against Germany together.
9 Germans defeat Russians at Minsk.
12 Mutual Assistance Agreement signed between Britain and Russia.
First German air raid on Moscow.
14 British occupy Syria.

1941

JULY

20 Stalin announces himself as Defence Commissar.

26 Roosevelt freezes Japanese assets in the USA and suspends relations.

27 First air raid on London for ten weeks.

28 40,000 Japanese troops land in Indo-China. Japan freezes US and UK assets.

31 Göring instructs Heydrich to prepare for 'Final Solution'.

AUGUST

1 Roosevelt announces an oil embargo against aggressor states.

5 310,000 Soviets captured after fighting ends around Smolensk.

7 US Senate extends its National Service to 30 months.

14 Roosevelt and Churchill sign the Atlantic charter.

18 Russians withdraw across the Dnieper River.

20 German siege of Leningrad begins.

26 German losses on Russian Front mount to 440,000, more than in the entire war before 22 June.

27 Pierre Laval is shot in an assassination attempt in Versailles.

30 Germans cut the last rail link between Leningrad and the remainder of the USSR.

Parks and botanical gardens, back yards and front gardens, school playgrounds, wasteland and, as the war went on, thousands of bomb sites were turned into allotments – about 1,400,000 of them by 1943 – for the growing of vegetables to feed the people. Many householders also managed to fit a hen house into their gardens which, by mid-war were producing something like 25 per cent of the country's officially acknowledged supplies of fresh eggs.

Another form of livestock that many people kept was the pig. A pig-keeping craze swept Britain, with thousands of Pig Clubs keeping pigs in back gardens, on allotments, behind pubs, feeding them on kitchen waste, much of which was collected in special pig food bins set up on street corners. At the same time, thousands of acres of agricultural land were brought back into use throughout Britain.

THE GRIM REALITY OF KEEPING HENS

Although she was just a very little girl in wartime Chingford, Mary Murphy remembers well how her mother dealt with the family's hens. 'My mother, who was a butcher's daughter from Kent, kept chickens at the bottom of our long, narrow garden among the fruit trees and blackcurrant bushes. She used to buy day-old chicks from Hoe Street market – Rhode Island Reds and White Leghorns – and we kept them warm with a light bulb in a cardboard box until they were old enough to go outside. I had to collect the eggs from the nest box in the chicken coop, still warm and smelling of the sweet straw. My father was too sentimental to kill them, but my mother had no qualms. I still have the axe. She would give the chicken to me by its feet, with its head hanging off and blood still dripping, to carry back to the house. I would hold it at arm's length because sure enough half way down the garden its wings would start flapping.'

12 August 1940: Children from Surrey elementary school being taught gardening during the holidays to keep them occupied and also to help them contribute to the war effort.

▲

10 July 1940: Boys from Five Ways Grammar School, Birmingham harvesting potatoes on a farm in Wales during World War II.

Children played a big part in all these different ways of providing food in wartime. 'Digging for Victory' became not only a useful patriotic activity for children, but also something that, as well as being interesting and exciting, was surprisingly life-enhancing. Even eating boiled cabbage in the school canteen at lunchtime could have something pleasurable about it when you knew that the cabbage came from the allotment outside on the playing fields and that it had been grown by your schoolmates.

Home-produced foods could have their drawbacks for children. Schoolgirl Joan Elliott, at home in Sheffield during the school holidays, remembers the awful smell of the hen food, which had to be boiled every day to stop it going off. She also remembers a particular Sunday lunch when the family had roast chicken. 'Is this Dora?' asked one of Joan's siblings, naming the family's favourite, rather elderly hen. There was a dreadful silence before the family went on eating.

Among the children who benefited most from 'Digging for Victory' were the thousands of children evacuated from big cities into the countryside. Not only did they discover that – in the often-quoted remark of a boy writing home to his mother – 'they have something called spring here', but they also learnt where food came from – milk from cows, not bottles, for instance – and how it was produced. Many of them enjoyed helping on the farm so much that when they grew up they left city life behind and returned to work in agriculture.

As more and more agricultural workers were called up, so thousands of young people had to be brought in to work on farms. While the well-known Women's Land Army, which included girls fresh from school at 14, worked on the land all year round, at harvest time many thousands of children, including whole classes from city schools, joined in helping to bring the harvest home. If these children were billeted on farms, then they might also spend much time feeding hens, looking after goats and even learning to milk cows and help, with supervision, in cleaning the milking parlour and looking after the cow shed.

For children living in towns and cities other splendid ways of helping with the war effort soon presented themselves. It was the newspaper magnate Lord Beaverbrook, appointed Minister of Aircraft Production in 1940, who made the word 'salvage' into a weapon of war that could be wielded by children as much as adults.

VEGETABLES AS PROPAGANDA

Potato Pete and Doctor Carrot were two figures created by the Ministry of Food as part of its propaganda campaign to boost wartime growth and consumption of vegetables. Both potatoes and carrots, which were widely grown on allotments and in gardens, featured in perhaps the Ministry's most notorious dish, Woolton Pie, named after Lord Woolton, the Minister of Food. Propaganda of another kind helped fuel the popularity of carrots among children. In order to keep secret their use of radar to warn them of in-coming planes, the Air Ministry prepared some spoof research in 1941 purporting to show that British fighter pilots had superior night vision because they ate lots of carrots. While the story may not have taken in the enemy for long, it was probably much more successful than any of the Ministry of Food's recipes in boosting the eating of carrots among British children.

▲

8 October 1940: Schoolchildren in Harrogate, with the help of their headmaster, started their own pig and poultry club. In this picture one of the young farmers holds one of the farm's geese.

1942: Miss Daphne Hubbard, a member of the Timber Corps, fells a tree at a timber camp in Bury St Edmunds, England. The Corps are helping in the war effort.

In a newspaper article published in July 1940, Beaverbrook asked the British public for aluminium to help make fighter planes. He had seen how the desperate need for fighter planes in the summer of 1940 had led to every crashed plane being taken to the Ministry's vast Metal and Produce Recovery Depot in Oxfordshire so that every reusable spare part could be salvaged. But, said Lord Beaverbrook, the planemakers were still not getting enough aluminium. Could the people help? Indeed they could. Housewives up and down the land began searching their cupboards for pots and pans to take to their nearest WVS depot.

In the end the government received a huge embarrassing amount of aluminium, much of it of little use in aircraft production. But Lord Beaverbrook's 'stunt', as it came to be called, had touched a chord with men, women and children. 'Salvage' became as important a word in the war on the Home Front as did the phrases 'Dig for Victory' and 'Make do and Mend'. Schools, children's comics, newspapers and magazines all encouraged children in their salvage-collecting efforts. *Good Housekeeping*, for instance, ran a Children's Salvage

◄

Metal pots collected by British women for use in the war effort.

Competition in 1943 which required children to enter designs for posters with a salvage theme, the prizes for which were Savings Certificates and Savings Stamps – and the chance for the prize-winning children to see their posters reproduced in the magazine.

Among the salvage schemes entered into with enthusiasm by children were those to collect metal, glass, including jam jars (provided they weren't being used as beer glasses in country pubs), paper, books (used to re-stock blitzed libraries and for keeping the services supplied with reading material), tins, rags and scraps of material (especially wool for battledress) and silver paper, all of which could be reprocessed or reused in some way. Even meat bones were useful, for they could be turned into aircraft glue.

The metal that children could gather included old bicycles, tricycles and pedal cars, prams, both real and toy, the metal tops of their mothers' scouring powder packs, and many battered and rusty tin toys. The latter, given the drastically reduced toy production during the war, could be a real sacrifice on the part of the child handing over a toy car or train.

Hundreds of thousands of children joined 'Cogs' corps, a nationwide scheme that turned children into 'cogs' in the great salvage-collecting machine. As *The Times* newspaper noted in 1941, the 'Cogs' scheme was based 'on the knowledge that all children like responsible, worthwhile work to do. Schools were asked to co-operate and most did.' There was a 'Cog' battle song, written by a WVS member, with a first line of 'There'll always be a dustbin', Cogs could win badges for collecting scrap and, for some corps, there were lapel badges, like the one in the shape of a cogwheel designed by a local woman for a corps in Kent.

1941

SEPTEMBER

1 Nazis order that all Jews in German-occupied areas over six years of age must wear a yellow star of David with the word 'Jew' inscribed.

2 First experimental use of gas chambers at Auschwitz.

19 Germans take Kiev.

24 First U-boat enters the Mediterranean.

26 German High Command records the capture of 655,000 prisoners in Kiev.

29 Babi Yar massacre – Germans kill nearly 34,000 Jews at Kiev.

OCTOBER

2 Operation Typhoon begins – the German advance on Moscow.

12 Thousands of women and children are evacuated from Moscow.

19 Stalin declares a state of siege in the capital and orders the inhabitants to defend their city to the last.

20 50 hostages are shot in Nantes, France, in retaliation for the assassination of a German military commander.

23 Walt Disney's full length feature '*Dumbo*' is released.

24 Germans take Kharkov.

29 Germans advance into Crimea.

30 Germans reach Sebastopol.

31 US destroyer *Reuben James* sunk off Iceland.

1941

NOVEMBER

13 British aircraft carrier *Ark Royal* is sunk off Gibraltar by a U-boat.

18 Operation Crusader, the British offensive in Libya, commences.

20 Germans take Rostov.

27 Russian troops retake Rostov.

DECEMBER

5 German attack on Moscow is abandoned.

7 The Japanese attack Pearl Harbor.

8 USA and Britain declare war on Japan.

11 Italy and Germany declare war on the USA. The USA declares war on Germany and Italy.

12 Hungary and Romania declare war on the USA. India declares war on Japan.

19 Hitler takes complete command of the German army.

22 Japanese launch a major invasion of the Philippines. 32,000 Jews are killed by the Germans in Lithuania.

25 Hong Kong surrenders after a 17-day siege. Over 3,000 people starve to death in Leningrad.

26 Winston Churchill becomes the first British prime minister in history to address a joint session of the US congress.

Apart from the great salvage business, there was another unexpected result from Lord Beaverbrook's call for aluminium for fighter planes. Spitfire Funds, in which people gathered together to raise money to pay for the building of new aircraft, with Spitfires (estimated by the Ministry of Aircraft Production to cost £5,000 each) the most popular, were a spontaneous reaction of the public to the call for pots and pans. Again, children were in the forefront of collecting money, often through their schools which ran Spitfire Funds of their own. And, according to the historian Angus Calder, in *The People's War*, it was a schoolboy who started the practice of paying for parts of aircraft when he sent a guinea (£1.05) to Lord Beaverbrook to pay for a Spitfire's thermometer. Beaverbrook immediately published a list of what it would cost people to pay for aircraft parts, from sixpence (two and a half new pence) for a rivet, to £2,000 for a wing.

While Beaverbrook's price list, if not actually plucked from the empty air, bore little relation to economic reality in the aircraft construction business, it was a portent of the savings boom that became such a feature of life in wartime Britain. In fact, saving money to help the war effort became an even bigger obsession with everyone, including children, than collecting salvage.

▶

1943: A housewife puts household items in marked sacks during a salvage scheme in Hornsey, north London.

A man and boy try to salvage a bicycle from the debris of a bombed house in London.

CHILDREN'S WARTIME SAVINGS SCHEMES

The War Savings Campaign, with its great theme of saving to bring victory, was an extension of the 1930s' National Savings Movement. Savings Certificates and Savings Stamps, which could be bought by children as well as adults, were two of the most important elements in the Campaign. Among the hundreds of thousands of savings groups organised during the war, many were in schools. Head teachers had a supply of savings stamps which pupils could buy with money raised outside school in a myriad different ways, sticking the stamps into their own savings stamps booklets. Larger schools might collect several thousand pounds a year in National Savings. In addition, children alerted, like their parents, to the value of saving for the war effort by the BBC's regular Sunday evening updates on saving schemes throughout the country, were well to the fore in all the special savings 'drives' such as War Weapons Week, Warships Week and Wings for Victory Weeks.

Many thousands of older children learnt the discipline of working together to help their country in its hour of need by way of such voluntary youth organisations as the Boy Scouts, Girl Guides, Boys Brigade and the junior wing of the Red Cross. Other young people, who if the war had not intervened, would still have been schoolchildren until they reached 15, found themselves doing paid adult work at 14. Although they could not legally join such organisations as ARP until they were 16, there was nothing to prevent 14-year-olds taking on other great responsibilities, filling the vacancies left by older men called up into the services.

The Post Office was an important employer of 14-year-olds. Although Post Office managers tried to ensure that their youngest employees got at least half a day's schooling a week, for very many children, the day they left school at 14 was the last day of their formal education. Many of them were employed as telegram delivery boys, riding on their bicycles through war-damaged streets to deliver telegrams. As there was really only one kind of telegram that got priority delivery during the war – the one from the War Office that contained the news that a husband or son was missing or had been killed – delivering telegrams became a truly terrible job for any 14-year-old.

From early 1942, when the government made an urgent appeal for young men to come forward to replace all the miners who had been conscripted into the armed forces, schoolboys volunteered for the coalmines but in numbers far too low to fill the gap. In 1943, Ernest Bevin, a Labour Minister, decided that compulsion was needed and began the thoroughly disliked scheme for

POPULAR CULTURE IN 1942

Popular Songs

White Christmas, by Bing Crosby
Moonlight Cocktail, by Glenn Miller
(I've got a gal in) Kalamazooo, by Glenn Miller
Tangerine, by Jimmy Dorsey

High-grossing films

Mrs Miniver, starring Greer Garson and Walter Pidgeon
Reap the Wild Wind, starring Paulette Goddard
Random Harvest, starring Ronald Colman and Greer Garson
Yankee Doodle Dandy, starring James Cagney
Road to Morocco, starring Bing Crosby and Bob Hope

JANUARY

1 Declarations of the United Nations signed by 26 Allied nations.
United States and Filipino troops fight the battle of Bataan.

20 SS leader Heydrich announces 'Final solution of the Jewish problem' to the Wannsee Conference.

21 Rommel's counter-offensive from El Agheila begins.

26 First American forces arrive in Great Britain, landing in Northern Ireland.

balloting boys as they reached the age for National Service, so that one in every ten became a Bevin Boy. In the last year of the war, 21,000 balloted Bevin Boys were working in the mines, along with 16,000 boys who had opted to work down the mines. Most of the Bevin Boys were 17 and many of them were middle-class boys who had hoped to join up and, with a bit of luck, fly fighter planes. Working down the mines may have been a terrible job, but it was essential work.

In early 1941, with the Blitz at its height and invasion all too likely, the Ministry of Information in cooperation with the War Office issued 14 million copies of a leaflet called 'Beating the INVADER' the main part of which was a message signed by the Prime Minister, Winston Churchill, in which he told the nation to 'STAND FIRM' and 'CARRY ON'. A few months later, with the war situation looking no better, young people were brought officially into the war effort, with all 16–18-year-olds being required to register for war service, whether in a youth organisation or a junior service.

CHARITY BICK, G.M.

The George Medal, awarded in recognition of acts of outstanding gallantry on the Home Front, was established by King George VI in 1940, the same year that the George Cross (the civilian equivalent of the Victoria Cross) was established. The youngest person to be awarded a George Medal during World War II was 14-year-old Charity Bick. Charity chose to lie about her age, saying she was 16 in order to get a job as an ARP Services Despatch Rider. She was awarded the George Medal for her extraordinary bravery during a very heavy air raid on Birmingham in February 1941. During the raid she not only helped her ARP warden father put out an incendiary bomb but also rode a bicycle a mile and a quarter through a heavy bombing raid to get a message to the ARP control post about another serious incident that had knocked out telephone lines.

The Air Ministry had already (in January 1941) formed the Air Training Corps (ATC), for boys aged between 16 and 18. This was the first state-directed, properly regimented youth movement ever organised in Britain. Thousands of boys who had spent the past months learning to identify, with the aid of illustrations on cigarette cards and outlines published in comics and newspapers, the aeroplanes in the air above them, while thrilling to the exploits of the RAF fighter pilots who had saved the nation in the Battle of Britain, were greatly attracted by the thought of being able to wear a proper RAF uniform, and joined up in their thousands. Within six months some 200,000 boys, all proudly wearing smart uniforms, were sitting at desks happy to study the mathematics and related subjects that most of them had found pretty boring at school.

3 August 1943: Workers at a Marmet pram factory in Letchworth, Hertfordshire, do their best to solve the shortage of baby carriages in Britain.

▶

'Britain shall not burn' 1940 (coloured litho).

16 July 1941: Flag signal training for British Sea Cadets in the Home Counties.

▼

The ATC example was quickly followed by the Army and the Royal Navy, who founded the Army Cadet Force and the Sea Cadets as their youth training corps. The War Office also scrapped the old Officers' Training Corps and replaced them with Junior Training Corps (JTC), or school cadet units, which boys could officially sign up for at 14, though many did so at 12, and which operated in schools under the auspices of the Army Cadet Force. One of the attractions of joining a school JTC was attending an annual camp at which the boys learned to use rifles, Sten guns and even Thompson sub-machine guns.

Fourteen-year-old boys could also join a Sea Cadets corps, which they could stay in until they reached 18, learning the skills needed to be a trained seaman in the Royal Navy or the Merchant Navy.

1942

FEBRUARY

2 President Roosevelt signs an order directing the internment of Japanese nationals in America and seizure of their property.
4 Japanese bomb Singapore for four days non-stop.
14 Japanese invasion of Sumatra begins.
17 Japanese invade Bali and bomb Darwin, Australia.
25 Princess Elizabeth registers for war service.

MARCH

18 Lord Mountbatten appointed Chief of Combined Operations.
22 Three-day battle begins in the Mediterranean.

APRIL

3 2,000 people killed in the Japanese bombing of Mandalay.
9 78,000 US-Filipino troops are captured in Bataan.
10 'Death March' of captured US-Filipino troops.
18 First US air raid on Tokyo and Japan by 16 B-25 bombers led by Colonel Doolittle.
24 Luftwaffe begin Baedecker raids on historic cities in Britain.

Not surprisingly, girls were not offered the same sort of national service opportunities as boys in 1939, and it was not until 1942 that the Girls' Training Corps (GTC), the Girls' Naval Training Corps (GNTC) and the Women's Junior Air Corps (WJAC) were formed to give girls pre-service entry training. Inevitably, perhaps, many girls, despite their smart uniforms, found themselves doing rather more tea-making, cooking and office work than fighting training, although they were introduced to the complexities of Morse code, radio communications, signalling and electronic engineering.

▲

1943: Boys from a mining village who are helping to increase Britain's coal output during the war, on their first trip underground.

▶

17 July 1943: Women's Junior Air Corps (WJAC) members attending a Girl's Rally at Belle Vue, Manchester, fix their hair before going to the funfair.

PLAYTIME

'Total war' did not mean there could be no playtime for children.
Rather, it meant that playtime was something to be enjoyed at home instead of
away from the home environment. Certainly, for many, the greatest playtime of all
– the annual holiday, usually to the seaside – became a thing to look forward
to when the war was over.

It was not just that many beaches were now out of bounds, hidden behind barbed wire, concrete anti-tank blocks and other anti-invasion devices. There was also the problem of how to get there. Petrol rationing kept family cars up on blocks in the garage 'for the duration', and all those posters at railway stations and elsewhere asking 'Is your journey really necessary?' made families think twice about leaving home.

Sports and games stopped being a regular school activity, sometimes because playing fields were taken over by air raid shelters or 'Dig for Victory' vegetable plots (with the vegetables grown by the children being used in the school canteen), but also because schools were not encouraged to have their children gathered together out-of-doors on playing fields. This was particularly so in those parts of the country most at risk from enemy action.

Front Line 1940–1941, a Ministry of Information booklet, published in 1942 and telling the 'official story of the civil defence of Britain, 1940–41', noted that the children of London became 'very expert shelterers and Blitz citizens. They made a practice of using as their special play-pitch the sites of their demolished homes, where they could on summer evenings in 1941, be seen soldiering with sticks and mounting guard in some symbolic play understood only by themselves.' The photograph accompanying the text shows four boys swinging round a decapitated lamp-post on both ends of a length of rope tied to it, using the piles of bricks scattered around them as jumping-off points. Probably the boys, like many others throughout Britain, made a hobby of collecting shrapnel from the streets and bombsites.

For many children, the best place for outdoor sports was in the street outside the house. With few, if any, cars about, streets were an ideal playground. Patricia Houlahan, who was eight when the war started, lived in heavily bombed Portsmouth throughout the war. Of Portsmouth's 70,000 houses, 63,000 were damaged in one way or another during the attacks on the city and its dockyards in 1940–41. Not surprisingly, none of Patricia's wartime schools offered outdoor sports at school, so she played often on the street.

▶

Three girls playing, part of a wartime crèche installed at Dallington, so that mother could work during the day to help the war effort.

1942

MAY

4 USA begins food rationing. Battle of the Coral Sea, first naval clash fought entirely with naval aircraft.

6 On Corregidor, US General Jonathan Wainwright surrenders his forces.

8 Battle of the Coral Sea ends as a tactical victory for the Japanese.

12 Soviet Army launch their first major offensive of the war and take Khartov in the Eastern Ukraine from the Germans.
1,500 Jews gassed in Auschwitz.

14 Women's Auxiliary Army Corps is established.

27 SS General R. Heydrich critically wounded in Prague by Czech Commandos.

30 RAF bomb Cologne in first of 1,000 night raids.

31 Japanese submarines infiltrate Sydney harbour to try to attack Allied warships.

JUNE

1 Germans bomb Canterbury in reprisal for Cologne.

4 Battle of Midway begins.

5 Siege of Sebastopol begins.

10 Nazis carry out massacre in the Czech village of Lidice in reprisal for the killing of Reinhard Heydrich.

12 Anne Frank receives a diary for her 13th birthday.

13 America opens its Office for War Information.

THE HAZARDS OF STREET PLAY

The Luftwaffe did not confine its activities to the hours of darkness, especially when they were making 'hit and run' raids on coastal towns and dockyards. Children playing in the streets became used to stopping their play long enough to try to identify the planes flying low overhead. Sometimes German planes were not what they seemed to be. Patricia Houlahan, playing in her Portsmouth street, vividly recalls one such plane. 'We were used to seeing bright yellow training planes in the air above us during the day,' she remembers. 'One day, we children playing in the street saw a bright yellow plane flying very low over us and did not take much notice. Then, it dropped a bomb on the nearby railway line and flew off.' The enemy had thought up a new way to disguise its planes. The children did not stop playing in the streets.

▶

Tending the Wounded
11 January 1941: A group of children in Worthing, Sussex have formed their own Air Raid Protection and first aid parties, with uniforms, casualty clearing stations and all the trappings of the grown-up world.

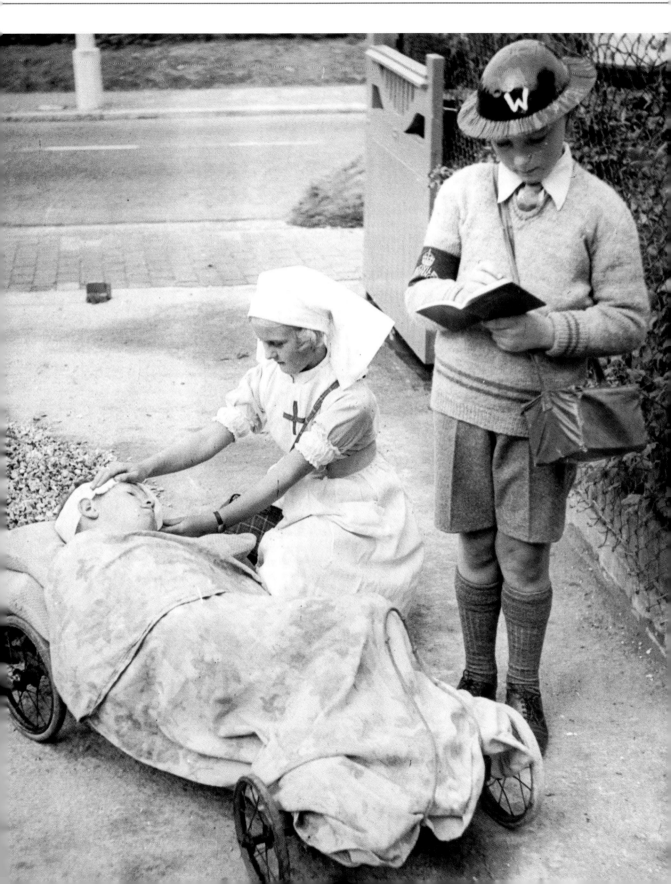

1938. The family at home, tuning in to hear the news on the radio. They have gas masks at the ready.

As going out after dark, even if only to go a few houses away to discuss homework with a friend, was difficult and even dangerous during the blackout, especially in the winter, most evening playtime was spent at home with the family. The centre of attention in most living rooms was the wireless set. Even though she was only an infant, living in Stevenage in Hertfordshire during the war, Annabel Rudland can remember to this day the way her father carefully positioned on the dial of her family's wireless the numerous paper dots that would allow him to tune in quickly to all the long-wave stations for the latest news of the war, at home and abroad. *'The wireless was huge, with twelve valves that glowed brightly and which needed constant renewing. Sometimes the noise and crackle of the long-wave stations was awful, but my father sat there listening carefully to the news from those far-off places.'*

The British Broadcasting Corporation (the BBC) was Britain's greatest provider of news, information, morale-boosting propaganda and – most important of all – entertainment during the war. As well as all the still well-remembered 'family' programmes such as Tommy Handley's *ITMA* (It's That Man Again), Richard Murdoch's *Much Binding in The Marsh*, Arthur Askey's *Band Waggon*, and *The Brains Trust* and light music programmes, many involving dance bands playing at such famous London hotels as the Savoy, the BBC produced numerous programmes especially for children.

Foremost among these was *Children's Hour*, which was taken off the air in September 1939 because the powers that be at the BBC considered it too lightweight for

wartime. It was pretty quickly brought back on the air and for the rest of the war, led by 'Uncle Mac' (Derek McCulloch) and others, was required listening for thousands of children. One of *Children's Hour*'s best-known young broadcasters was the King's eldest daughter, 16-year-old Princess Elizabeth, who made a short broadcast to the children of Britain and the Empire from Windsor Castle in October 1940. The princess finished her talk by calling her sister Margaret to join her at the microphone to say goodnight.

It was not long before toy and game manufacturers began giving their products a patriotic wartime flavour. Wooden jigsaw puzzles, printed in bright colours, were particular favourites, especially with boys, who enjoyed putting together pictures of British fighter planes in the air over England's green and pleasant land or, as the war progressed and British troops began operating abroad, battle scenes with outcomes favourable to the Allies.

Girls – and their mothers – spent a lot of time knitting, using up scraps of wool to make stuffed toys for babies and infants, and dolls with up-to-the-minute clothes, such as the uniforms of the men's and women's services, for older girls. French knitting, done on a wooden cotton reel with four small nails hammered into the top, was also popular with girls. Even though she was only little, having been born in 1939, Mary Murphy remembers spending many hours at home in Chingford, Essex, making place mats, pot holders, tea cosies and egg cosies out of her French knitting.

Board games, played round the family table, were another popular play activity. While *Ludo* and *Snakes and Ladders* were always family favourites, other board games based on Home Front themes such as the work of ARP wardens, fire-fighters and others also appeared from Britain's toy and game manufacturers. Games like *Battleships* took on a new dimension in wartime, and extra fun could be got out of a dartboard with a picture of Hitler's face pasted on it.

Boys like collecting things. Bits of shrapnel were very popular – you could compare the size of your pieces with those of friends at school the day after a bombing raid. Then there were cigarette cards, which now put their subjects on a war footing, replacing the portraits of cricketers and other sportsmen popular in the 1930s with things like gas masks, accompanied by instructions on how to put them on, or home protection advice. Also very collectable were cap badges from servicemen, including, after 1942, those worn by American servicemen. There were great dangers in collecting, especially for children exploring in the grounds of munitions factories or on testing ranges, but also on bomb sites where unexploded bombs might lurk.

Children's publishers, despite wartime economies which meant that paper, in short supply anyway, was also of poor quality, soon swung into wartime mode. Leading children's writers, like Richmal Crompton, who had been delighting children – and their parents – since the early 1920s with stories about a mischievous boy called William Brown, quickly began putting their characters into wartime settings. Captain W. E. Johns, whose Flight Commander Bigglesworth, known to all as Biggles, had been flying in a daredevil kind of way since the early 1930s, put Biggles into stories set in Norway and during the Battle of Britain.

While paper restrictions meant that comics, like adults' magazines, were much reduced in size and page extent, those that did survive – and several pre-war favourites, like *Tiger Tim*, did not – also turned to war times themes for the adventures of their favourite characters, as did the heroes and heroines of such newspaper comic strips as *Rupert* (in an English national paper) and *Oor Wullie* and *The Broons* (both of which appeared in Scottish papers). *Dandy*'s regular character, the amiable giant Desperate Dan, put his weight behind the war effort, turning drainpipes into pea-shooters to bring down enemy aircraft and skimming across the sea flat stones large enough to take out enemy warships.

◀

Children in a street in south London sorting shrapnel, anti-aircraft shell fragments, which they have collected as their contribution to the national war effort.

1942
JUNE

21 Rommel captures Tobruk.
25 Eisenhower arrives in London.

JULY

3   Germans take Sebastopol.
5   Soviet resistance in the Crimea ends.
6   Anne Frank and her family go into hiding.
9   Germans begin a drive towards Stalingrad in USSR.
22 First deportations from the Warsaw Ghetto to concentration camps. Treblinka extermination camp is opened.

AUGUST

7   British General Montgomery takes command of the Eighth Army in North Africa.
12 Stalin and Churchill meet in Moscow.
16 Polish-Jewish teacher, Janusz Korczak, refuses Nazi offers of sanctuary and follows a group of Jewish orphans into Treblinka death camp.
17 First all-American air attack in Europe.
19 Allied forces raid Dieppe, France.
23 Massive German air raid on Stalingrad.
30 Battle of Alam Halfa – Rommel sustains heavy losses.

1942

SEPTEMBER

3 Fierce desert battle as RAF and New Zealand soldiers attack Axis supply lines. A German attempt to liquidate the Jewish ghetto in Lakhva leads to an uprising, the Jewish youth movement helps to plan the operation.

13 Battle of Stalingrad begins.

24 First female SOE agents are parachuted into occupied France.

OCTOBER

5 German eyewitness reports SS mass murder.

7 UN Commissioner to investigate war crimes announced in London and Washington.

18 Hitler orders the execution of all captured British Commandos.

26 Battle of Santa Cruz – US attack on large Japanese fleet.

NOVEMBER

11 Germans and Italians invade unoccupied Vichy, France.

13 First sea battle of Guadalcanal.

19 Soviet counter-offensive at Stalingrad begins.

26 The movie, *Casablanca*, premieres at Hollywood Theatre in New York City.

Publishers of boys' comics, including *Rover*, *Wizard*, *Skipper* and *Hotspur*, all brought war themes into their pages, including German spies, secret codes and, in *Hotspur*, a teacher at a boys' public school laying down his life for the British Secret Service. *Dandy* and *Beano* introduced specifically wartime characters into their publications. *Dandy*, for instance, had 'Big-hearted Martha, our ARP nut' and *Beano*, whose favourite enemy comic character was Musso da Wop, a 'big-a-da-flop' whose generals issued spaghetti to tie their soldiers' boots, also made fun of Adolf Hitler and Hermann Goering by way of characters called 'Addie and Hermy, the Nasty Nazis'.

When US servicemen began arriving in Britain in 1942 they brought with them, as well as apparently endless supplies of candy, their comics. Now British children began speaking American slang and thrilling to the exploits of a new and very different set of comic-book heroes, such as the supercop Dick Tracy (sporting a two-way wrist TV) and the amazing Superman, with his X-ray vision and ability to fly through space.

Outside the home, one of the most popular children's leisure time activities of the war years was 'going to the pictures'. At the outbreak of the war, the government, assuming an immediate bombing onslaught on Britain, closed all cinemas. It was soon realised that the effect of this on national morale was catastrophic, and cinemas were reopened within weeks. In fact, cinema provided everyone, young and old, with their greatest escape from the war. It was estimated that three-quarters of the British adult population considered themselves to be cinema-goers during the war, buying between 25 and 30 million cinema tickets every week. As for Britain's children, they were even more avid cinema-goers than adults, with a great proportion of children going to the cinema more than once a week.

▶

1944: A US soldier helps some children with their skipping. He is watched by his comrades in a town street in the south of England, lined with equipment awaiting shipment to France.

While most small children went to the cinema with their mothers, or with older siblings, as more and more mothers, especially from the working classes, took on jobs during the war so more and more children went by themselves. The Ministry of Information, noticing the great popularity of the cinema among children, focused their short information and propaganda films shown in cinemas on a wide age-range. Many people remember the wartime

documentaries and Ministry of Information 'shorts' with particular pleasure.

While many of the most popular children's films of the war years – *The Wizard of Oz*, *Bambi* and *Fantasia*, for instance – were American in origin, with the films of Walt Disney being well to the fore in the popularity stakes, especially with younger children, there was also plenty of home-grown film-making talent in Britain, much of it in the hands of the great cinema

◄

1942: A van belonging to the Ministry of Information travels the country stopping at villages to show mainly documentary films.

JUST ANOTHER MOVIE

Both as an escape from reality and as a way of coming to terms with it, the cinema was of great value to wartime children. When 13-year-old Kenneth Jones, at home in Croydon during the school holidays in early 1940, got caught up in an air raid, he not only had a great story to take back to school in Devon, he also had a way of dealing with the perilous situation in which he found himself. 'I was traveling home from London when the sirens started. The bus was obliged to stop and discharge its passengers. There was no air-raid shelter close, so we just stayed in the street while, above, the Germans were coming in to bomb Croydon airport. They were engaged by Hurricanes and a dog fight developed right over our heads, just like in the movies! I couldn't wait to get home to tell my friends how lucky I had been to have a front seat watching two German planes going down in smoke.'

mogul J. Arthur Rank. Older children, of course, took as much pleasure as grown-ups in the musicals, romances and war films that made up a large proportion of the output of wartime film studios, both British and American.

Most cinemas changed their programmes at least twice a week, and there was always more than just one feature film on the programme, plus an interlude from the Mighty Wurlitzer, the massive theatre organ that had been introduced in picture palaces in the 1920s and remained a feature of cinemas, except the very smallest, until the 1950s.

1942
DECEMBER

1 Gasoline rationing begins in USA.
16 Soviets defeat Italian troops on the River Don in USSR.
20 Japanese bomb Calcutta for the first time.
31 Battle of the Barents Sea between German and British fleets.

POPULAR CULTURE IN 1943

Popular Songs
Paper Doll, by The Mills Brothers
Sunday, Monday or Always, by Bing Crosby
Pistol Packin' Mama, by Al Dexter & His Troopers
That Old Black Magic, by Glenn Miller
The musical *Oklahoma* opens on Broadway

High-grossing films
For Whom the Bell Tolls, starring Ingrid Bergman, Akim Tamiroff and Katina Paxinou
The Song of Bernadette, starring Jennifer Jones
Stage Door Canteen, starring Cheryl Walker, William Terry, Marjorie Riordan, Lon McCallister and Margaret Early
Star Spangled Rhythm, starring Bing Crosby and Bob Hope

Rank's Odeon and Gaumont cinema chains ran Saturday morning cinema clubs specially for children, with tickets on sale at just a few pence. While much of the fare shown at cinema club mornings was American comedies, Westerns, serials and cartoons, there was also a sprinkling of films from a part of Rank's empire called Gaumont-British Instructional. After the war, Mary Field, who was a director of Gaumont-British, put her experience with the cinema clubs to good purpose when she set up a children's films division within the Rank organisation.

One popular leisuretime activity among older children that took on a new meaning in wartime was the youth group or youth club. Although many youth clubs were forced to close when war was declared, often because their young leaders were called into the services, the government was quick to mobilise those, such as the Boy Scouts and Girl Guides and the Boys and Girls Brigades, that were left. As early as 1938, Lady Reading, founder of the WVS, was in close (and secret) contact with the headquarters of the Girl Guides, asking for lists of Guides prepared to help the WVS with its local evacuation arrangements.

◀

15 March 1941: Although thousands of children have been evacuated from the town, many children are still to be seen playing at 'hellfire corner' in Dover, which has been taking the brunt of the German bombing raids.

During the war, Boy Scouts and Girl Guides and other youth groups were to prove their value to the war effort in many ways. Some of those ways, such as Girl Guides leading crocodiles of newly arrived evacuee children to their billeting officers or Boy Scouts staying in camp while helping to pick fruit for jam-making, were more fun than dangerous. But those Girl Guides who offered first aid help in ARP posts and Boy Scouts who got on their bikes to deliver messages between ARP posts and the police in front-line towns and cities, were often working in highly dangerous conditions.

BADGES WITH A DIFFERENCE

Boys and girls who joined the Boy Scouts and Girl Guides in peacetime, planning to earn an armful of badges for a wide range of indoor pursuits and outdoor activities, found themselves working for a very different kind of badge. For the Boy Scout intent on doing his bit in wartime there was a National Service badge to be won, while for Girl Guides, the badge to work towards was the War Service Badge, for which extra annual stripes could be earned. While many of the ways in which the badges could be earned involved the use of peacetime skills — erecting tents, weeding allotments or shopping for the blind, for instance — many more, such as distributing gas masks, directing traffic during blackouts (having already helped paint white stripes on kerbs and lamp posts so that pedestrians and motor traffic would notice them in the blackout), helping in first aid and ARP posts and, if they were old enough, being motorcycle messengers or telephone operators.

1943

JANUARY

1 Frank Sinatra appears at the Paramount, causing 'bobbysoxers' to flood Times Square.

10 Soviets begin an offensive against the Germans in Stalingrad.

13 Helmut Schenk becomes the first man ever to use an ejection seat.

14- 24 Casablanca conference between Churchill and Roosevelt. Roosevelt announces that the war can only end with an unconditional surrender from Germany.

27 First bombing raid by the USA on Germans at Wilhelmshaven.

FEBRUARY

2 Germans surrender at Stalingrad in the first big defeat of Hitler's armies.

9 Shoes are rationed in the United States.

11 General Eisenhower is selected to command the Allied armies in Europe.

18 Nazis arrest White Rose resistance leaders in Munich.

22 Allies make a commando raid on Myebon.

25 RAF begin round-the-clock bombing in Tunisia.

28 Commando raid ruins German atomic weapons plant at Telemark in Norway.

Annual holidays away from home became almost impossible for most families during the war. One way round this problem, which also helped with the major wartime problem of having enough workers to bring in the harvest, was to organise harvest camps for town children. Started in a small way at the beginning of the war, there were, by the summer of 1943, more than a thousand camps in England that could accommodate 63,000 children during their summer school holidays – and get the vital food harvests safely gathered in.

The government, all too well aware of the need for children to get a break away from the day-to-day restrictions and deprivations of wartime and to get out in the fresh air and sunshine as much as possible, also developed a scheme to encourage people to take 'Holidays at Home'. Local councils throughout the country were urged to provide concerts and other entertainments in public places, especially local parks, which were carefully kept as attractive-looking as possible, given wartime conditions and the fact that many public spaces were ploughed up for allotments.

Truth to tell, there was little more that the government could do than to 'encourage' people to take time off and enjoy leisure activities. It was up to parents to do whatever was possible for the children. And, also truth to tell, most children in Britain got on with their lives during the war much as they would have done in peacetime. As Patricia Houlahan says now, 'Most of my friends and I were not aware of the horrors of the war. We did not notice the absence of 'frills' and got on with things, including playing and entertaining ourselves.'

▶

18 August 1940: Inhabitants of a bomb-damaged London suburb sunbathing amongst the ruins.

15 March 1941: Unevacuated children play in the streets of Dover in south-east England in spite of the fact that it is one of the towns in 'hellfire' corner.

Jack Haley (1898–1979) as the Tin Man, Bert Lahr (1895–1967) as the Cowardly Lion, Judy Garland (1922–1969) as Dorothy, Ray Bolger (1904–1987) as the Scarecrow and Frank Morgan (1890–1949) as the Doorman to the Emerald City in The Wizard of Oz, 1939.

CHILDREN AND THE WORLDWIDE WAR

*The war beyond Britain's shores had far-reaching effects on children,
at home and abroad. Even before the war started a steady trickle of children
began coming into Britain with their families to escape the increasingly punitive
actions of the Nazis in Germany and Austria against non-Aryans, especially Jews,
who were stripped of civil, cultural and economic rights.*

Jewish children were thrown out of state schools in Germany and Austria, which was annexed by Germany in March 1938, later in that year. Because there was no private school system in either country, this meant that Jewish children were deprived of all schooling.

The trickle of Jewish refugees, especially children, from Germany and Austria became, if not a torrent, then certainly a steady stream after the violent 'Kristallnacht' attacks on Jewish property throughout Germany on 9 November 1938. The British government reduced its strict immigration rules to allow Jewish children between the ages of 5 and 17 to come into Britain from Europe, but placed quite severe restrictions on them in an effort to ensure that they would not become a tax burden on the country and that their stay would be limited, with 'ultimate resettlement' (ideally in Palestine) the goal to be aimed at by refugee agencies.

Thus began the 'Kindertransport' scheme that brought some 10,000 children to safety in Britain between December 1938 and the outbreak of war in September 1939. They came by train, crossing the Dutch border out of Germany and arriving from Holland at the English ports of Harwich and Southampton. The last train to leave Austria crossed the border with Holland on the day war was declared.

◀

World War Two Allied Nations: 18 May 1940, Betty Malek, aged three, with her bags and toys on arrival in London from Antwerp, Belgium. Antwerp has been bombed by German aircraft and hundreds of people made homeless.

1943

MARCH

15 Germans recapture Kharkov.
16 Battle of the Atlantic reaches climax with 27 merchant ships sunk by German U boats.
26 Battle of Komandorski Island

APRIL

4 Allies Bomb Naples, Syracuse and Sardinia
19 Warsaw Ghetto uprising, 60,000 Jews killed.

MAY

13 German and Italian troops surrender in North Africa.
15 *Batman* appears on screen for the first time in the US.
16 Jewish resistance in Warsaw Ghetto ends.
    The Dambuster raids by RAF 617 squadron on German dams.
22 Allies win battle of Atlantic.

JUNE

1 Eden announces Empire casualties for the first three years of the war – 92,089 killed, 266,719 wounded.
2 Russians bomb Kiev and Rostov as Luftwaffe bombs Kursk.
10 'Point Blank' directive to improve Allied bombing strategy issued.
11 Himmler orders the liquidation of all Jewish ghettos in Poland.

1943

JUNE

13 Looney Tunes animated short *Porky Pig's Feat* is released in US theatres.

19 Goebbels claims Berlin free of Jews.

20 RAF starts 'shuttle' bombing raids.

JULY

5 Germans begin their last offensive against Kursk. Naval battle breaks out in Kula Gulf, North of New Georgia.

9 Allies land in Sicily.

19 Allies bomb Rome.

22 Americans capture Palermo, Sicily.

24 British bombing raid on Hamburg.

25 Mussolini arrested.

27 Allied air raid causes a fire storm in Hamburg, killing 42,000 German civilians.

29 Evacuation of 1 million civlians from Hamburg.

AUGUST

6 Battle of Vela Gulf.

11 Germany begins night evacuation of Sicily.

13 Roosevelt and Churchill meet at Quebec Conference.

16 Heavy air attacks on Japanese airfields on New Guinea.

17 US daylight air raids on Regensburg and Schweinfurt in Germany.

24 Himmler is named Reich-minister of the Interior.

For many of the Kindertransport children, the first experience of life in Britain was within a hastily set-up camp, perhaps in run-down First World War transit camps or in tents on isolated farms, even, in one case, in un-used greenhouses on a Nurseries site. Eventually the children were billeted with foster families, which, as with Britain's own evacuee children, were sometimes good, comfortable and caring, and sometimes the reverse, and found places in schools. When the hastily, ill-conceived internment scheme for 'enemy aliens' was begun, more than a thousand Kindertransport 16-year-olds and above were even put into internment camps for a time.

British schoolchildren, seeing yet another kind of stranger in their classes, tended to accept Jewish refugee children in much the same way as they accepted the evacuees from cities and industrial areas, with indifference, tolerance, or irritation, depending on how many of these children there were, and how much difference it made to their own lives. It was not until after the war, when the full, horrifying extent of the holocaust was revealed that children and their parents began to see the Jewish children from Europe in a new light.

As for the Kindertransport children themselves, some stayed in Britain and some moved on to the United States, Australasia and, eventually, Palestine and, after 1947, Israel. Almost all of them, when they boarded the trains to safety, left behind parents, siblings and other family members and most of them never saw their parents again. They were orphans, not just of the war, but of the holocaust, too.

▶

Jewish refugee children from Germany and Austria arrive at Liverpool Street Station in London, 5 July 1939.

Another group of evacuees to Britain came from the UK overseas territory of Gibraltar. Several thousand Gibraltarians were evacuated first to North Africa in mid-1940, then in a merchant shipping convoy that brought them, in appallingly over-crowded conditions, to England from July 1940. Few of the children among them could speak English and during the next four years in which they lived with their families in hostels in London, they were taught there rather than attending English schools.

PAYING FOR SEAVACUATION

With so many calls on their money supplies to contend with, the government could not make the CORB scheme free. For most of the parents who queued outside the CORB London office – set up, with probably quite unintended irony, in that pre-war 'Temple of Travel', Thomas Cook's stylish Mayfair headquarters – there would be costs to meet. True, their children would be given free passage on the ship, but parents would have to make the same size of contribution towards their maintenance that would have applied if they had been evacuated in Britain. A means test would be used to assess, on a sliding scale, the size of parents' contributions. If the child had been to a fee-paying school at home, parents would be asked to pay £1 a week towards the child's upkeep, plus an extra £15 towards the cost of travel.

Although things were very quiet on the Home Front during the early months of 1940, invasion from Europe still seemed so likely that better-off parents, who could afford the £15 that a one-way ticket by sea to America could cost, began stepping up the arrangements that many of them had been making since before the War started to send their children overseas. At the same time, with the situation in France looking very threatening indeed, the governments of Australia, New Zealand, Canada and South Africa, as well as America, repeated earlier offers of hospitality in even stronger terms than before. In May 1940, the British government decided to accept these offers and put in hand a government-sanctioned scheme to evacuate children overseas.

A Children's Overseas Reception Board (CORB) was set up to arrange such evacuations and to receive the names of children whose parents wished them to be registered for the scheme. Over 211,000 applications, many of them from families who could not have afforded the cost themselves (£15 was the average monthly salary of the great majority of British men in 1940), were received within a fortnight of the CORB scheme opening.

CORB eventually sent just over 2,664 children overseas, most of them to the United States and Canada, but more than 400 of them, with their escorts, to Australia. One reason for this low number was the lack of suitable ships; another was the lack of enthusiasm for the scheme expressed by Winston Churchill, among others, partly because of the bad effect the scheme could have on national morale, but mainly because of the dangers involved: German U-boats were prowling the Atlantic seaways in great numbers. The government could not guarantee the safety of the children and nor would it agree to making any commitment to bring them back at a particular time. In the end, nearly 20,000 of the 'seavacuees', as children sent abroad came to be called, were sent overseas, most of them to Canada, under private arrangements made by their families.

The 'seavacuation' scheme was dealt a dreadful blow in September 1940 when the SS *City of Benares*, lead ship in a convoy of merchant and passenger ships in the Atlantic, was hit by a torpedo and sunk. There were one hundred children on-board, including 90 CORB children being sent to Canada. Eighty-one children perished. The CORB scheme was stopped shortly after, although the government continued to grant exit visas to parents wanting to make their own arrangements for their children.

▲

9-year-old Michael Corrie, a refugee from England, takes the ferry to Ellis Island in New York, 1941. Evacuated from Bedford, Corrie arrived in New York without an entry visa, since his father had forgotten to give it to him. The Ellis Island Immigration Station is in the background.

When 14-year-old Kenneth Jones left his English school to return home to Chile at the end of 1940, he was accompanied by his mother. Kenneth recalls an eventful start to his voyage to Chile. 'We missed our convoy and had to spend the night on board ship – the night of the first massive bombing of Liverpool docks. We were locked in our cabins with the ship shuddering and rocking with the all-night bombing. Mother was quite calm and therefore so was I. It was just as well we missed our convoy because that was the one that received a great U-boat attack and the *Empress of Canada*, full of children, was sunk.'

When the war was over and the seavacuees returned to Britain, they came back, well fed and well clothed, with strong North American accents, and with an even greater liking for all things American, from music and movies to comics, candy and bubble gum, than their G.I.-influenced contemporaries who had spent the war years in Britain.

The same could not be said for many of the British children caught up with their parents in overseas countries when the war began. While the rules of war meant that accredited diplomats and their families were granted safe passage out of countries with which their own governments were now at war, British workers overseas and their families were not so fortunate. Everyone who has read J. G. Ballard's *Empire of the Sun* will know what happened to the British in Shanghai during the war; even worse was experienced by those British caught up in the capture of Singapore in 1942.

◄

From left to right, young refugees Dennis Collins, John Fenn and Doreen Davenport speak to their parents back in England from the NBC Radio City Studios in New York, 9 February 1941.

1943

SEPTEMBER

3 Allies begin the invasion of Italy.
9 Allied landings at Salerno and Taranto.
11 Germans occupy Rome.
12 Germans rescue Mussolini.
16 Salerno mutiny.
23 Mussolini re-establishes a Fascist government.
30 Danish Jews rounded up by Gestapo and Danish Nazis.

OCTOBER

13 Italy declares war on Germany.
2 Japan opens infamous Burma-Sian railway built by POW labour.
26 Germany repatriates 790 wounded POWs to Britain.

NOVEMBER

18 Large British air raid on Berlin.
28 Roosevelt, Churchill and Stalin meet at Tehran Summit Conference.

DECEMBER

2 Conscription for active service introduced for Hitler Youth.
11 Heavy US air raid on Emden kills 1,000.
18 German war criminals sentenced to death at Kharkov war crimes trial.
24 Soviets launch offensives on Ukraine.

POPULAR CULTURE IN 1944

Popular Songs

Swinging On a Star, by Bing Crosby
Don't Fence Me In, by Bing Crosby and the Andrews Sisters
I'll be Seeing You, by Bing Crosby
I Love you, by Bing Crosby
I'm Making Believe, by Ella Fitzgerald and the Ink Spots

High grossing films

Going My Way, starring Bing Crosby
Meet Me in St Louis, starring Judy Garland
Thirty Seconds over Tokyo, starring Spencer Tracy, Van Johnson, Phyllis Thaxter, Robert Walker and Robert Mitchum
Hollywood Canteen, starring Joan Leslie, Robert Hutton, Dane Clark and Janis Paige

JANUARY

1 Soviet troops advance into Poland.
14 Russians launch new offensive around Leningrad.
17 British launch main attack on Japanese 'Golden Fortress' in the Arakan, Burma.
27 Leningrad relieved after a 900 days seige.
29 Luftwaffe penetrates London.
800 USAAF bombers hit Frankfurt.

▲

Poster, DON'T LET THAT SHADOW TOUCH THEM.....BUY WAR BONDS, featuring three children playing as menacing shadow of swastika surrounds them.

▶

18 August 1940: An old man and a young boy, both refugees from Belgium, arriving at a station in London.

On the whole, however, the children of Britain were saved from the worst that war could do. Britain was not invaded and did not have to be fought for street by street, mile by mile, often by children (12-year-old members of the Hitler Youth movement fought the soldiers of the Red Army in the streets of Berlin in 1945), as happened to many of the countries of Europe. There was no mass starvation – indeed, many people agree with the food writer Marguerite Patten, who worked as an adviser with the Ministry of Food during the War, that, on the whole, Britain's children were fed a more basically healthy and nutritious diet between 1939 and 1945 than they were before and since.

VICTORY AND AFTER

The sense among many people that Britain was fighting a losing war, widespread in the first two or three years, gave place to a guarded optimism once the RAF had begun to seriously attack the German industrial heartland and once America, catapulted into the war by the Japanese attack on Pearl Harbor in December 1941, was suddenly 'over here' in large, confident numbers, giving candy to children, cap badges to boys and shampoo and silk stockings to their older sisters.

Children at play in the counties of southern England soon began to notice how a huge army was taking shape around them. Eight-year-old Janet Foord, playing in the woods round her home in Epsom, Surrey, watched the woods becoming increasingly filled with soldiers, their equipment and the tents in which many of the soldiers lived. The Allies were amassing a great invasion force, hiding it from German surveillance planes in every wood and under large trees in southern England – or so it seemed to Janet and her friends.

When D-Day eventually came and the invasion of Europe began in June 1944, Janet and everyone else at school thought the war would be over soon. In fact, for children like her, living in the counties surrounding London, the war was to get every bit as dangerous as it had been for years past, as the Germans unleashed their V1 and V2 weapons on Britain. The immediate result of the V-weapons attack was another, albeit quite small, evacuation from the cities in the firing line.

Long before the rocket attacks had ended, those mothers and children who had spent years as evacuees, began to return home in considerable numbers, even to homes that were in cities very much in the V-weapons' line of fire. In many towns, officially organised de-evacuation schemes began in December 1944; soon hundreds of women and children were on the move, in trains organised by local councils, from 1939's Reception Areas back to what had been the Evacuation Areas at the outbreak of war.

▶

Children sit down to a victory party at a V-shaped table, given by residents at Kentwell Close, Brockley in south London.

1944

FEBRUARY

1 Polish underground execute chief of Gestapo in Poland.
15 Allies bomb the monastery at Monte Cassino.
16 Germans counter-attack against Anzio beachead.

MARCH

4 Soviet troops begin an offensive on the Belarussian Front.
15 Second Allied attempt to capture Monte Cassino.
18 British drop 3,000 tons of bombs during an air raid on Hamburg.
19 German forces occupy Hungary.
24 Battle of Berlin is over.

APRIL

10 RAF drop a record 3,600 tons of bombs over Northern France.
13 British take Nunshigum Hill, Burma.
14 Russian troops take Tarnopol.
28 749 US troops are killed in Exercise Tiger at Start Bay, Devon, England.

MAY

9 Russians capture Sebastopol.
11 Allies attack the Gustav Line south of Rome.
23 Allies launch massive breakout at Anzio.
25 Germans retreat from Anzio.

By March 1945 plans were complete for the return of evacuees in the south of England and industrial Midlands, for those whom accommodation was available.

In London, where the public shelters were closed and the bunks taken out of the Underground in April, as many as eight dispersal points were set up, at which arrivals would be fed and given a great welcome. In the event, most of the de-evacuation trains, organised by the 1500 local authorities who had received telegrams telling them to 'operate London return plans' on 2 May, arrived half-empty because people had already de-evacuated themselves and their children.

Even the Channel Islands, still officially in German hands, began to welcome their children home from late autumn, 1944. More than one Channel Islands evacuee returned home with their names written in large letters on their suitcase or bag; their foster parents, seeing how much the child had changed and grown in the five years since leaving home, thoughtfully gave their birth parents a chance of recognising their children, from whom there had been no photographs and very little communication at all since they had waved them off in 1940. For some weeks, returning evacuees to the Channel Islands had to live on Red Cross parcels, so bad was the availability of food in the islands.

Eventually, back in Britain, the rocket attacks stopped, the Allies reached Berlin, and the second world war of the twentieth century was over. The first great celebration came on VE (Victory in Europe) Day, 8 May 1945; then, on 14/15 August 1945, VJ Day celebrated the end of hostilities in Japan and the Far East.

◄

Crowds celebrating VE day on the streets of London, 8th May 1945.

1944

JUNE

1   BBC sends coded message to French resistance to say that an Allied invasion of Europe is imminent.
5   Allies enter Rome.
       The German navy's Enigma messages are decoded by the Allies.
6   D-Day landings begin.
7   Allies liberate Bayeaux.
13 First German V-1 rocket attack on Britain.
15 US invades Saipan.
27 US troops free Cherbourg.

JULY

3   Battle of the hedgerows in Normandy.
       Soviets capture Minsk.
18 Hideki Tojo, the prime minister of Japan resigns.
20 Hitler survives an assassination attempt.
25 Operation Cobra – US breakout from Normandy.

AUGUST

1   US troops reach Avranches.
       Warsaw uprising begins.
2   Turkey ends diplomatic relations with Germany.
15 Operation Dragoon begins.
20 Russians attack Romania.
25 Liberation of Paris.
30 Germans start pulling out of Bulgaria.
31 Soviet Troops take Bucharest.

1944

SEPTEMBER

4 Finland and Soviet Union agree to a ceasefire.

13 US troops reach the Siegfried Line.

OCTOBER

2 Warsaw uprising ends.

NOVEMBER

8 USAAF start 72-day bombing of Iwo Jima.

DECEMBER

16 The Battle of the Bulge in the Ardennes.

27 Soviet troops beseige Budapest.

1945

JANUARY

1– Germans withdraw from
17 the Ardennes.

16 Nazis begin to evacuate from Auschwitz.

30 *Wilhelm Gustloff* passenger ship sunk in Gdansk bay.

FEBRUARY

4 Yalta Conference between Churchill, Roosevelt and Stalin opens.

7 Germans blow up floodgates on Ruhr.

13 Dresden destroyed after Allied bombing raids.

For Britain's children, celebrating the great victory often took the form of street parties, with the children gathered round tables brought out from houses up and down the street. Every mother would either make a dish for the party or provide a precious pot of jam, something from their tea ration or even a pat of butter or fat that could be used to bake cakes, jam or lemon tarts and biscuits. Marguerite Patten, who worked for the Food Advisory Division of the Ministry of Food during the war, recalls being told by children that they ate ice cream for the first time in their lives at a Victory street party.

It was a great shock to many when, once the bells had stopped ringing and the flags and bunting had been taken down, there was very little relaxation of many of the wartime rules and regulations. Most vexatious of all was the fact that food rationing, so far from being ended, was continued and even increased: bread, never rationed during the war, had to be in 1946, largely because of a poor grain harvest in Britain and a world-wide shortage of wheat.

STEPS TO DE-RATIONING

Bread, which was the last food to be rationed in Britain, was also the first food to be taken off the ration, in July 1948. It was followed at the end of the year by jam, marmalade (often made during the War from a concoction based on apples and carrots, with not an orange in sight), syrup and treacle. Everyone had to wait nearly four more years for another food, this time tea, to be de-rationed, and it was not until February 1953 that the food every child, and most adults, had been waiting for, sweets, came off the ration. Photographs of children queuing eagerly outside sweets shops appeared in the newspapers, and there were a few more seven months later when sugar was de-rationed. It was not until July 1954 that ration books could be thrown away, when meat was the last food to be de-rationed.

Children wearing skull caps adorned with the Victory V sign (donated by the British War Relief Society of America) at the Stoughton Nursery School in Guildford.

POPULAR CULTURE IN

1945

Popular songs

Sentimental Journey, by Les Brown and Doris Day
Rum and Coca Cola, by the Andrews Sisters
Until the End of Time, by Perry Como
On the Atcheson, Topeka and the Sante Fe, by Johnny Mercer
My Dreams are Getting Better All the Time, by Les Brown

High-grossing films

The Lost Weekend, starring Ray Milland
The Bells of Saint Marys, starring Ingrid Bergman and Bing Crosby
Leave Her to Heaven, starring Gene Tierney, Cornel Wilde and Jeanne Crain
Spellbound, starring Ingrid Bergman and Gregory Peck
The Son of Lassie, the second Lassie film, becomes the first ever to be filmed using Technicolor Monobook method
First cartoon featuring *Casper the Friendly Ghost* is shown

In September 1946, a full year after the war's end, photographs of Aberdeen schoolboy Martin Wagrel's mother filled the front page of the local newspaper, the *Weekly Journal*, photographed as she did her daily shopping, the family's ration books (including Martin's) in her shopping basket. Sited centrally on the page is the inevitable photograph of Mrs Wagrel standing in a long queue outside a shop. The caption under every other photograph tells whether Mrs Wagrel must use points or coupons to buy the food, whether it is rationed or not and – perhaps most significantly, how its price compares with what it was a few years before – badly, of course, with the cost of one day's supply of greens for the family being the same as a week's supply, 'time was'.

While food, its rationing and availability was a long-term, post-war problem, of much more immediate concern to children in the weeks and months after the war was the emotional problems that all too often arose when father returned. Although the government had been planning for demobilisation since late 1942, hoping to avoid the economic and social problems that had bedevilled the country after 1918, it was impossible to plan for the emotional turmoil that could be aroused in a child when a long-absent father came home. As Janet Foord remembers, as an only child she had had her mother's undivided attention during the war. 'I felt very jealous of my father when he came home on leave – and when he came home for good.'

◄

Three London children enjoy the thrill of purchasing lollipops as the Hackney sweetshop well stocked with sweets as rationing becomes a thing of the past.

In Janet's case, the jealousy subsided quite quickly – helped a little by the fact that her wartime request for a bicycle, always greeted with the stock reply, 'After the war…', was now answered and she got a new bike. But for many children, less well-circumstanced than Janet's family, or perhaps bombed out from their homes, the reality of their father's return was made worse by the fact that jobs and housing were both in short supply.

Many a father returned home to be greeted by his family, bombed-out from the house he had left them in, at the door of a 'pre-fab' – a factory-built, pre-fabricated house that was supposed to be replaced within years, if not months, by something more permanent, but which was quite likely to be still lived in at the turn of the century by the returned serviceman and his wife, now retired and very happy to be in their snug little bungalow. Despite committees and mid-war planning, the country returned to peacetime industry very slowly, so that building new houses – and providing the jobs to do the building – took a long time to get going.

The same issue of Aberdeen's *Weekly Journal* that had followed Martin Wagrel's mother on her shopping expedition in September 1946 also reported on the Town Council's efforts to house the 150 'most necessitous cases' among the many homeless families in Aberdeen. 'They will be moved into Hayton Camp – one of the main wartime training depots in the town – just as soon as the Army moves out…. Electric light, water, cooking and washing facilities are to be laid on, and it is believed that the new homes will be better than what is being occupied in many parts of the city at present.'

1945

MARCH

Anne Frank dies of typhus fever in Bergen Belsen concentration camp.

3 Finland declares war on the Axis powers.

9/ US B-29 bombers attack
10 Japan.

19 Hitler issues his Nero decree.

30 Soviet troops capture Danzig.

APRIL

1 US troops encircle Germans in the Ruhr.

18 German forces in the Ruhr surrender.

28 Mussolini is captured and hung by Italian partisans.

30 Adolf Hitler commits suicide.

MAY

2 German troops in Italy surrender.

7 Unconditional surrender of all German forces to the Allies.

8 VE day (Victory in Europe).

9 Herman Göring is captured by the US Army.
Norway arrests Quisling.
Red Army enters Prague.
Occupation of the Channel Islands ends.

23 Heinrich Himmler, head of the Nazi Gestapo, commits suicide while in British custody.

BUILDING A NEW BRITAIN

The assertion by the Minister of Labour, Ernest Bevin, at the height of the War in 1943 that the one way to stop moral and social disaster after the War was to build enough houses for every family, could not be acted upon with any speed until the War was over. Planning for the future could start, however, and resulted in 1944 in the passing of the Town and Country Planning Act. The purpose of the Act was two-fold: to replace the housing destroyed in the Blitz and after, and to make the country's towns and cities fine places to live in, with plenty of green, open spaces. The New Towns Act of 1946 brought in the concept of 'New Towns', either completely new or built as satellites of existing towns. The first new town in Britain was Stevenage in Hertfordshire, which got the go-ahead in November 1946.

While it would be a long time before every family in the country was properly housed, the first steps in the provision of what the Beveridge Report, back in 1942, had called a 'security net' for all, were taken. In June 1945, one of the last acts of the war-time government, now a 'Caretaker' government led by Winston Churchill, brought in the Family Allowances system, starting with the payment to families of five shillings (25 pence) a week for every child after the first one. In the following month, Churchill's Conservative government was defeated by the Labour Party in the first General Election since the war began.

Thus, the creation of Britain's Welfare State, planned in the midst of war, was firmly begun in the first weeks of peace. For many, however, the Welfare State's birth can be dated from 5 July 1948, when the new National Insurance scheme and the National Health Service both came into operation. For the nation's children, a date of more immediate concern was the raising of the age at which they could leave school to 15. This was not much of a shock, because it had been planned before the war and was prefigured in the 1944 Butler Education Act, along with a major reorganisation of the education system in England and Wales.

On the whole, Britain's parents could be justified in hoping for a better world for their children. As for the children of the war years themselves, they can look back on what Janet Foord remembers as the fun and enjoyment of the 1950s. The pretty young princess who had talked to them on the *Children's Hour* programme during the war and had still managed to look lovely both in her ATS uniform as she helped repair Army trucks in 1945 and as she walked down the aisle of Westminster Abbey at her wedding in 1947, was now Queen Elizabeth II.

▲

Headlines in British newspapers telling about end of candy rationing, extra petrol for summer, lights on again in England, off-coupon day in London stores, cheaper railway fares and other good news headlines.

Children standing in the yard of a new prefabricated home.

People were talking about a New Elizabethan Age – there was even a new, glossy magazine for girls called *New Elizabethan*, children had got unrationed sweets back, even if only a couple of months before the new Queen's coronation, which took place in June 1953, and there were lots more attractive clothes for children and young people in the shops. There were 'bobby-soxers' in America and quite soon there would be a totally new kind of older children called 'teenagers' everywhere. The war years would soon become just a memory – and not an all bad one.